For "the" Bob
& international
Lions game.
all the,
Best !

Jerry
Clarke

Published and Printed by BookMaster's Inc.
2541 Ashland Road, Mansfield, OH 44905

Cover and art work by Cindy Pendleton
Pendleton Fine Arts

Chitina Past
ISBN 0-9722934-0-X

This journal is dedicated to the memory
of Miss Rubye Karo, PhD.,the only
English teacher worth a damn who
ever taught in Cordova.

To all the people who listened while I
regaled them of my teenage perils in Chitina,
here's a thank you for your patience.  To
the many wonderful friends who said
"you oughta' write a book", here it is.
To those who helped, to Carole Bodey,
who edits so well, to Bookmasters for
its splendid guidance, my full thanks.
And to the love of my life, Joy, how
can I thank you enough.

                              L. C.

# CHITINA PAST

## The Late '40's

**Larry Clarke**

# C O N T E N T S

Remembering Chitina

# ILLUSTRATIONS

**Cover and Art by Cindy Pendleton**
**Pendleton Fine Arts**

## REMEMBERING CHITINA

These are stories about people and events
in the remote village of Chitina, Alaska, when I
was a teenager. My father was a bush pilot and
the time was the late 1940's. The ghost town
(or village) of Chitina lies next to the Copper
River, some one hundred miles inland from the
Gulf of Alaska. Many references are made to
the Kennicott Copper Mine and the Copper River
and Northwestern Railway, both of which closed
in 1938, ten years before the time of my
reflections. The people about whom I have
written include both Indians and oldtimers.

Two of the principal characters living
there were O. A. Nelson, who owned the townsite
of Chitina, and Melvin Chase, the man who
operated the Chitina Cash Store for O. A.
It is one thing to face new and completely
different experiences as a teenager living in
Alaska, and yet another to recall what happened
50 years ago. Time has a way of smoothing over
the rough spots of the past and delivering a
softer version of most events.

It is said that history is "in the
writing". However, this journal is not a
history. It is just a collection of memories
and events which have stayed with me for a long
time. If any of this proves to be interesting
to you, that will be enough for me.

Larry Clarke

## HOW WE GOT THERE

My family moved from New Jersey to Alaska in 1947. We were part of that great, post-war movement in America which countless families underwent in the late '40s. It was not our first move as a family but it became our final one. The effect of the relocation and my wonder at this new country, Alaska, has never left me. How rapidly time has flown and what terrific changes have occurred since then! I have gone from a teenager to a grandfather since we arrived at Cordova on July 11, 1947, and have often wanted to start that rich experience all over again.

Our first three years in Alaska were unique. Dad was a bush pilot and, along with my mother and sister, lived in the remote village of Chitina, while I boarded in Cordova going to high school.

Dad became a beginning bush pilot at the age of 38 and worked for Merle "Mudhole" Smith and his Cordova Air Service. After having him fly in the Cordova-Prince William Sound area for almost three months, "Smitty" moved my folks up the Copper River to operate the air service out of Chitina. Chitina is 250 road miles from Anchorage.

The air service area is vast and included the drainages of both the Copper and Chitina Rivers, which surround the Wrangell Mountains. It was so large that it is served by at least five air services today. In the 1940's, with antiquated equipment, rare maintenance, and unusual customer requests, the renaming of Dad's employer to Cordova "Ground" Service was often appropriate. Being a pilot then was a tough job, but the challenge must have been extremely rewarding to Dad. Respect, love and

1

high regard were accorded to him by everyone.
The man blended with the function.  In fact,
they were inseparable.  Looking back, I can see
how it couldn't have been any other way.  My mom
called my dad, actually he was my step-father,
either by his last name, Steelman, or "Pappy",
his nickname.  I called him Uncle Hildreth,
which name I had used before he and mom married.
I know that when Dad had to leave "Smitty" and
the air service in 1949, it was with  many
regrets,  regardless  of  any professional
improvement, or the fact that he was going to
work for money again.  During the last four
months he flew for Smitty, his only compensation
was being allowed to buy food at the Chitina
Cash Store on the air service account.
Unfortunately, Smitty had run out of cash.
     Mother was always a busy person and,
having been in food service and restaurant work
all her life,  developed a social outlet for the
few hardy bachelors in town who partook of her
home-cooked  suppers  each  night.  Her cooking
ability prompted her to reopen the old
Commercial Hotel under a new banner, SPOOKS
NOOK, in each of the summers of 1948 and 1949.
That old, rundown building had 20 bedrooms and
offered  three  family-style meals every day
until just after Labor Day.  Mom used the money
she earned to board me at the Windsor Hotel in
Cordova, where I finished high school.
     At its zenith, Chitina was only a road
junction at a railroad stop.  It was never a big
place.  There was an Indian village nearby, a
post office, two hotels, a good-sized Alaska
Road Commission Camp, the general store, a pool
hall, the Arctic Brotherhood Hall which doubled
as a movie theatre, workshops, barns, and about
30 houses and cabins.  The town was put there to
serve the Copper River and Northwestern Railway.
The railroad went eastward to the

Kennecott Copper Mine, and the road going north out of town was called the Edgerton Cutoff. It led to the Richardson Highway near Copper Center. Chitina was 131 miles from Cordova by railroad and, coincidentally, exactly 131 miles by road from the seaport village of Valdez. Chitina had changed greatly by the time we arrived nine years after the railroad had shut down. In fact, Chitina had become a ghost town. There were only about a hundred people living there, most of whom were Indians. The Chitina Cash Store had survived the railroad, and a combination drugstore/post office sat across the street next to the road out of town. During World War II, the Alaska Road Commission had relocated its operation to Glennallen, near the junction of the Glenn and Richardson Highways. It had left a Caterpillar tractor behind for emergency work on the road, and the airstrip located near Mile 5, north of town.

I enjoyed two different lives. One as a high school kid boarding in Cordova. The other as the visiting son working for his mom during the summer. Thus I was somewhat lost each year when I came home from school. However, in spite of all its remoteness and sparse population, Chitina still held many things for me to do. Not that Cordova wasn't new and strange too, because it was, but the routine of going to school and spending most of my time there made it more familiar than Chitina, so that the happenings in Chitina seem to have impacted me more intensely. It was a great place for a teen-age boy!

When I was ready to go back to Cordova from Chitina after Christmas vacation in my junior year, several things happened which delayed my return. There was a shortage of operational aircraft, Dad had injured himself, and the weather had turned very, very bad. Unless Dad had a reason for flying to Cordova

3

with either a fare, switching planes, getting maintenance, or filling in for another pilot, the way for me to get back to school was to wait for the mail plane or some other Cordova-originated flight to come to Chitina. School was due to start the day after New Year's Day, but between Christmas and New Year's Day my dad accidentally sliced his knee crosswise while building a dog sled, so he had to stay off his feet for almost two weeks. In addition, when the planes were finally due to fly, the weather turned sour over the eastern part of Prince William Sound and the Copper River Valley.

One weather report we heard through Gulkana Weather (CAA Radio) stated that the accumulated snow at Valdez over a 48-hour period was twelve feet! This was January in 1949.

Dad had been using a drawknife to smooth the willow runners on a dog sled he was making for Nig, our lone pet husky. The knife caught on a little knob and he automatically braced the butt end of the runner with his knee, but the little knot of wood gave way and the sharp blade cut right through Dad's clothes and went into his bent knee a good half to three-quarters of an inch just below his kneecap.

Mom quickly slapped the cut together with a butterfly tape and it eventually healed smooth as silk. But before all that, Dad compounded the injury by having a drink of whiskey. It was about -25 below outside where he had been working and at least 75+ above inside. The combination of the cut, the marked difference in temperature and the whiskey put him into shock.

I can still see Pappy reaching up to the top shelf of the kitchen cabinet to get the bottle of whiskey for a "shot". Mom had already gone down to the drug store to radio Cordova to tell them that Dad was laid up. If she had been there, with her training and experience, she wouldn't have let him have his "shot". So, he drank some whiskey and not ten minutes later was flat on his back in shock. Cold, shivering, aching! He felt so bad that he became a helpless patient for the next two days!

All the while, I wanted to get back to Cordova. I was a Junior in high school, passionately set on making the basketball team, and I had to get back to school to do this. Day after day went by with no air traffic. It was the dead of winter, cold and dark! Things looked gloomy regarding my return trip!

One night, sometime after the fifteenth of January, we were all sitting in the living room, reading and talking, when Mom and Dad started reviewing how circumstance had probably happened for the best after all. They said that I was a real big help and could probably get a job with O. A. Nelson or "Chase" at the Chitina Cash Store, and since so much school had gone by, it wasn't much use for me to go back to Cordova anyway. I would have missed too much schoolwork. Thus, they decided that I could stay out of school that semester and go back again in the fall.

I was crushed!

My folks just sat there and teased me until they finally laughed and eased my pain. I'll never forget that episode.

By the time I did get back to Cordova for the second semester of school that same year it was January 23rd. I was three weeks late!

I will never forget going back to Cordova after my last summer in Chitina. It was the fall before my senior year of high school. Mom had refined the Spooks Nook operation and I thought my bullcooking for her was superior. I had grown to my full height and was probably as cocksure and wiry as any 16 year-old could ever be. All summer, I had forced myself to run or

5

fast walk everywhere so that I would be ready
for the basketball season.  A couple of days
after getting back to Cordova, Jimmy Webber and
I ran up to the top of 2,100 foot high Mt. Eyak
and then slid and ran back down.  It only took a
couple of hours.  We were insufferable, thinking
we were super athletes!

The stories and incidents included in this
journal have been running around in my head for
many years.  I jotted notes about some of them
years ago.  Recently, I finally put all my notes
and thoughts together.

## GOING BACK AGAIN
### -August 13, 1960

On a vacation camping trip into the Copper
River country, I pulled into the Liberty Falls
campground the first morning from Anchorage
and wrote on my note pad, "The morning is cool,
clear, and remarkably serene. An ever-pounding
beating and rustle, of water falling, hums in my
ears. A pinewoodsy smell surrounds me. These
falls and camp are a utopian refuge!"
Later that same day, I drove the last ten
miles into Chitina. Not back to the old Chitina,
where I had lived in the late forties as a boy,
but to a Chitina grown visibly older and
rundown. The town had regressed.
My first encounter with someone I had known
brought mixed feelings. Charlie Jacobsen was
older, much thinner, and looked a lot like O. A.
Nelson had looked ten years earlier. I didn't
talk to him, just saw him.
Shortly afterward, I came upon a trio of
natives near a fishwheel, located on the bank of
the Copper River near the foot of the rock wall
where the old cable car had once sat, two
hundred feet high on a cliff. One of them was
Big Susie King, grown old and gray, dressed
just the same, in pants and shirt with a red
kerchief tied over her hair. Another was Mr.
Marshall and the third was a man with a .30-.30
rifle. They had gone there to chase bears away
from their fishwheel.
The man with the rifle was Charley
Phillips!
The last time I had seen Charley was on
the morning of July 4th, 1949. I had been
perched on top of the Spook's Nook hotel
trying to fasten an American flag over the
front of it to help celebrate Independence Day.
Charley had been sitting in the back seat of

7

Deputy Marshal Nels McCrary's black sedan and was being driven to the Anchorage jail for murdering Hank Bell the night before. Charley had believed that Hank had been dallying with Charley's wife and, while under the influence of much whiskey, had called Hank out at the cabin Hank shared with Mr. Marshall. Hank had run from the cabin toward Charley. Charley fired his .30-.30 at Hank. The slug had torn straight through Hank, right through his heart. As he collapsed at Charley's feet, the bullet had gone through the open cabin door and lodged in the pillow on which Mr. Marshall's head had been resting.

These three Indians, down by their fishwheel, seemed older to me than time itself, and poor by our hurry-up modern standards. But they were true survivors. Big Susie had been a little girl when the copper hunters canoed up the Copper River, near the turn of the century. Mr. Marshall appeared even older, but still carried himself with care and great dignity. When I spoke with the three of them, he acted as their leader. Charley Phillips was armed with a .30-.30, which was probably the same rifle with which he had killed Hank Bell eleven years earlier. Mr. Marshall was the same man who had been the cabin mate of Hank Bell. It was beyond me to tell them who I was, that I had been a boy in their village a generation earlier. But my feelings even then were that, if given enough time, the land and the man-made ravages inflicted on this remote village and these people would disappear. I believed the real owners of the land were these native people, and they would eventually prevail.

The maximum penalty for murder committed by an Indian during Alaska's territorial days was only 20 years. Charley Phillips had gotten out of prison early. For good behavior!?

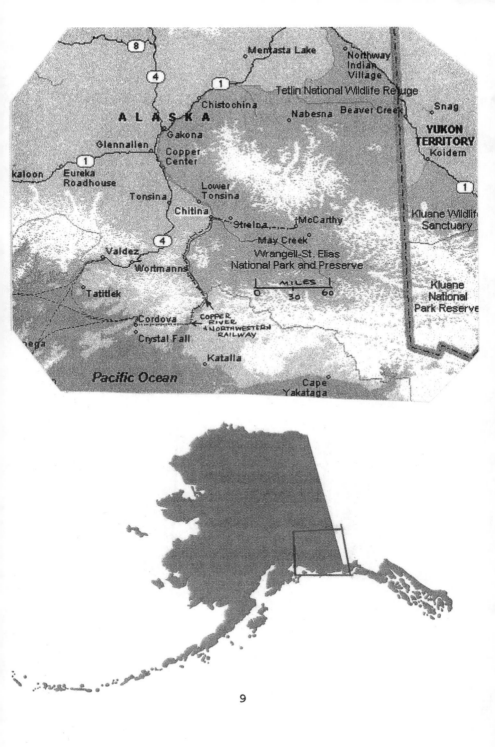

9

# BREAKFAST WITH BILL
## A Roustabout
### Summer of 1949

O. K.  It's time to get up!"

I came to, not completely awake, lying on a cot in a strange room with an old geezer hollering down at me.  He slowly came into focus, as I stared up at him.  I remembered.  He was Bill Berry.  We were in McCarthy and it was time to get up and get ready to fly back home to Chitina.

As I got dressed and packed, Bill brought a big glass of milk into the room where I had been sleeping.  He announced, "It's time for breakfast!"

I took the glass from him but as I brought it to my lips I could see that it wasn't moving like real milk or like powdered milk either.  There certainly weren't any cows in McCarthy.  And the white stuff was much too thick to be real milk.

"What is it?", I asked.

"This is the food that kept me going when I was carrying the mail to Chisana *."  Then Bill paused.

I stood there, looking at the glass filled with the strange-looking white stuff and then started to smell it.

"Drink up!"  He growled at me.

With plenty of misgivings, I upended the glass and drank it straight down.  Down the hatch.  It was just as thick as it appeared.  It was real sweet and milky. I drained the glass and then handed it back to Bill Berry.

"What was it?"  I asked.

"Canned milk, an egg, and plenty of sugar!"

*  pronounced shoo sha na

11

I almost gagged.

Bill Berry went on to explain that when he was a young man, he had carried a hundred-pound pack over Skolai Pass from McCarthy to Chisana. It was fully loaded with food to sell to the gold miners.

"Sold everything for a dollar a pound! Made two or three hundred dollars every trip!" I was only 16 years old then but I easily figured out how advanced his math had been and wisely held my tongue. It was a good story.

We had spent the previous day driving from Chitina to McCarthy in an old speeder on the abandoned Copper River and Northwestern Railway. The speeder was a converted Model T Ford touring car which still had some of its original canvas flapping from its roof. My mom had let me go to McCarthy with Bill Berry and Mr. Paul Wilhelm, who was the caretaker of the closed-down Kennecott Copper Mine. The next day, I would fly back to Chitina with my dad when he'd return while making his regular Chitina-McCarthy mail run.

We made this trip in the summer of 1949, eleven years after the C. R. & N. W. R. W. had shut down, and the railroad bed wasn't in very good shape. But it was good enough for us to get the speeder up to 40 miles an hour in some stretches.

We had started out early in the morning, and the first thing we had to do was cross the Copper River in a cable car. This sounds pretty fancy but it really wasn't. The railroad had left a cable system with a work box hanging from it, measuring three by six feet. The contraption was powered by a Model A Ford engine which took 12 minutes to pull the car across the river to the McCarthy side, using the reverse gear. The trip was faster coming back to the Chitina side in a forward gear. Getting up to the cable car platform wasn't easy either. A person had to climb a beat-up, old boardwalk which had been fastened to the rock cliff overlooking the river. The elevated loading platform, where the engine was located, was about 200 feet above the surface of the Copper River. However, I thought the platform was at least a mile above the water.

It took three round trips going back and forth across the river before we finished loading the speeder with the supplies we were taking to McCarthy. The sixty-mile trip would take all day. We weren't in a great hurry because we had a special job to do along the way. We had to repair the single-strand telephone wire between the two villages. The wire was supported by a succession of tripods. It seemed as if most of the tripods had fallen down. We would ride a little way and then stop. We set up tripods all morning and half of the afternoon. Fortunately, the closer we got to McCarthy the more the tripods were still standing. Thus our speed picked up as we went along.

I remember three things vividly about that trip other than the novelty of it all. They were the Kuskalana Bridge, a trackwalker's shack at Strelna, and our stop at Long Lake.

Crossing the Kuskalana Bridge can be a daunting experience even today. The high, wooden trestle bridge makes a long, slow curve across the Kuskalana River. Although the bridge is paved today, it still only allows a one-way passage and still is just as high. The fact that this wooden structure is over 80 years old should be a cause of much concern. Just how long do wooden bridges last?

Then we came to Strelna. There was an old trackwalker's shack there. All of those small railroad shacks were built exactly the same and all had been painted barn red with white trim. The two gentlemen, I was with, made sure I examined the old hut carefully and then told me

13

what I was actually seeing.

They both walked into the cabin and all around it and then one of them said, "Yep, that's it. You can see it."

With that, they showed me where a brown bear had climbed in through the window. The men pointed out the deep gouges it had dug into the clapboard siding with its claws, how the window had been muscled askew by its big body, and then how it had torn its way out through the door of the shack.

"That's the way they do it," my companions said. "They never go out the same way they go in. It doesn't matter whether the building is a cabin or a house, as long as there's two ways to enter. They go in one way and leave out the other."

It has been hard to forget the two sets of claw marks which were gouged into the side of that old trackwalker's shack.

Later on, we stopped at Long Lake. From our vantage on the railroad track we could look way down to the lake which was slowly being covered by the shadows of the lengthening day. Bill and Paul then pointed at something I wouldn't have noticed, but which they had obviously seen many times before.

There were two brown bears swimming the length of the lake far below us. We could see their wakes and just their heads showed above the waterline. No one was living at Long Lake then and its shoreline wasn't an easy place to climb down to. Those bears were doing exactly what I would have been doing if I had lived there. I'd have gone swimming! In the summertime! Just for the fun of it!

We followed the railroad track until we finally arrived at the Kennicott River. We crossed it in a little, hand-powered cable car. There was an old truck on the McCarthy side. After loading it up, we drove to the Wilhelms'

house. Marge, Paul Wilhelm's wife, met us and
gave us big soupbowls of fresh raspberries and
cream. We talked for a little while. Soon
after eating that delicious dessert, Bill Berry
and I went to his place and bedded down for the
night.

After I had breakfast with Bill the next
morning we drove up to the airfield where my dad
flew in from Chitina. Got a chance to meet the
other residents of McCarthy and then we flew
back to Chitina. I remember flying past
Gilahina Butte on the way and counting over 300
Dall sheep. There were only ewes and lambs. No
rams.

I never saw Bill Berry, Marge, or Paul
Wilhelm again. After finishing high school the
next year in Cordova, it was another three years
before I made it back to Chitina again. That
was only for a short, four-day visit with O. A.
Nelson before returning to college in Fairbanks.

As I recall, the cable car operation
across the Copper River had ended by the time I
came back, so it was all the more memorable for
me to have had a chance to go across the river
back in 1949.

At least in reverse!

# BIG SUSIE

It would be hard to imagine the Chitina of my teenage years without Big Susie King. The last time I saw her was in the summer of 1961, in a scruffy little bar which Neal Finnesen had opened behind the old Arctic Brotherhood Hall. She dominated the drinkers and was being stood to free beer by the tourists. Susie claimed to have finished eleven by the time I left the bar.

That was twelve years after my last summer working as a bullcook for my mom in the Spooks Nook Hotel she and O. A. Nelson had opened.

Big Susie King was between 60 and 65 years old. Describing her might serve to reveal more about the little community of Indians which had been in Chitina before the railroad and the copper mine came to make changes.
Susie was an imposing woman, tall and erect, nearly six feet tall. She had high, full cheekbones, wide-set brown eyes and strong, even white teeth. Usually she dressed in pants and a skirt of some kind, plus a shirt under a button sweater. Her head was never bare as she always wore a scarf over her black, gray-flecked hair. Mother grew to know her fairly well, and Susie confided many things to her. Mom would talk about Susie and most of my writing about what Susie said and did have came from my mother. Susie told her that she remembered there were no white men in the area when she was a little girl. She said she saw the first ones when they came up the Copper River from the coast to start the railroad.

Big Susie was absolutely honest and frank with no artifices. Physically imposing, she worked laboriously during the summer tending her fish wheel, splitting and drying countless

salmon, and carrying loads of the half-dried fish tied into bales on her back up the 200-foot, zig-zag path to the top of the sandy cliff and then another half mile to the village.
There she sold her fish to the Donahues who ran a pressure-cooking, canning operation as part of their missionary cause.
In the late 1940's, when Alaska was still a territory, only natives could own and operate fish wheels. It was evidently a conservation regulation set up by the federal government to help the Indians continue their way of life.

Big Susie explained that the way her people had caught salmon, when she was a little girl, was far different than the fish wheel of the 1940's. Small dams, known as weirs, were fashioned out of willows and placed in narrow places in the small, feeder streams. Mainly fishing was done with individual, hand-held, dip nets, also made of willow. There was no, non-stop, paddlewheel fishing done back then.
Susie's fish wheel was successfully located at the best possible spot on the Copper River and lay directly east of the village. It was located on the other side of the two hills which sit between Town Lake and the Copper River. Her wheel was renowned locally. It caught more king salmon than any other wheel did. During one 24-hour period, the churning wheel caught over 400 king salmon!

Susie's brother, Patty King, looked exactly like Susie. They could have been twins for all I or anyone else knew. I remember, many years later, seeing an obituary in the Anchorage Times which said that Patty had passed away at the age of 76. He and Susie were certainly alike. They were vital, strong, and very nice. Patty had worked as a heavy equipment operator for the Alaska Road Commission.

I mention him because I don't believe either Susie or Patty ever had children. Susie was supposedly married to a George Brickel, who had been a track foreman on the railroad before it closed in 1938. Both Susie and Patty King should have had kids because they both were kind to many children and were such find and generous people.

Susie made a beaver hat lined with ermine, for my little sister, Mary-Linda. It was beautiful! Susie fashioned it as a full, head-shaped helmet covering my sister's brow and coming all the way back of her head, completely covering her neck. After my sister died, my mother gave this beautiful fur hat to the Alaska Museum in Juneau.

A first look at Big Susie King would probably have shown her as just another poor Indian woman who was shabbily dressed, living in a hopeless environment. But, knowing her, and realizing all she did, and how she coped with the many changes and the obvious ravages her people had suffered, revealed that she possessed a great and resilient strength. After all, she and her people have been surviving in a harsh and magnificent land for thousands of years before the white man came. Their infinite patience will see them through this current blending of two cultures.
Would any of us pampered white people be able to do half as well, if we were invaded by an alien culture, as Big Susie and her people were.

When I think of strong, indomitable people, survivors against all odds, I think of Big Susie King and the Chitina people.

# HIDDEN FEAR

Airsickness was an overpowering problem for me when I was young! Every airplane trip was preceded by the knowledge that I would soon be overcome by turbulence and disorientation and I would get airsick again!

The first time that I got airsick happened a couple of years before my treks started between Cordova and Chitina. It was classic for its inconvenience. Dad, and his nephew, Preston Force, and I had driven from English Creek in south New Jersey to Lynchburg, Virginia, to buy a two-seater Luscombe airplane, then fly it back to the Atlantic City Airport.

We arrived and found the plane at the Lynchburg Airport. The next morning we got ready to take off, leaving Preston on the ground to drive our car back to New Jersey. As we flew away, Preston waved up at us...and then we couldn't see him anymore as we swept off to the northeast.

I remember how it all looked as we flew over Chesapeake Bay, the wide Delaware River, all the little towns, and white, crushed-shell roads, and the lacework of waterways overlaying south New Jersey and even our home in English Creek. Dad flew over our house and wagged our wings to Mom and Mary-Linda.

One outstanding sight I remember was Monticello, Thomas Jefferson's lovely estate, which we flew directly over. The often-pictured, white rotunda sat in the middle of a wide, well-groomed grassland, surrounded by lush greenery. We were probably only 500 feet high and the sight was breathtaking! Everything was bathed in gorgeous bright sunshine.

Another outstanding sight was the unending panorama of dark-green mountains which

20

continued mile after mile toward the southeast.
These ranges were gathered in belts of white and
pastel colors and seemed as unspoiled as the day
they were first seen by whites several centuries
before.

Unfortunately, we had to land after only
being airborne for ten minutes when I was
airsick for the first time in my life. That
malaise continued for most of the time I flew to
Chitina and back from Cordova. It was not until
I learned to fly in the army several years
later that my airsickness totally
disappeared.

# BIG JAKE

The late August morning was chilly with wisps of fog coming off Town Lake. It was easy to get away, by just walking out the back door of the old hotel with my fishing pole. Mom didn't need me for any chores, so I was happy to run out and go fishing by myself for awhile. Between Chitina and the double-humped hill next to the Copper River, was the prettiest lake a person could envision. It was so peaceful and clear that the bushes along the edge of the water were perfectly reflected in the undisturbed surface of the water. Town Lake was almost perfectly round and that morning was ringed by a railroad track which allowed the locomotives to turn around. It was along the south side of the lake that my feet led me. A trail, almost a road, left from the abandoned track, took me farther and farther around the lake.

I wandered counterclockwise around the lake, alder trees and berry bushes were on my left next to the lake. High on the hill to my right, a movement near the three little shacks caught my eye. Someone or something was causing a commotion in one of the huts. I stopped and stood quietly by the cut of the hill, unmoving, hidden from sight, and looking upward. Suddenly, with a whoop and a cackling laugh, a little Indian woman exited one of the cabins. She jumped up and down in front of it, and then turned about six or seven somersaults down the hill. As I watched in amazement, she leaped to her feet and ran back uphill to the cabin from which she had burst. Just as she got there, the door frame of the cabin was filled by a giant of a white man. The woman grabbed at him. He grabbed at her, and then they disappeared back inside the cabin.

I stared up at the cabin on the hill for a long while and then finally continued around the lake. I just kept wandering along, not thinking about fishing. Instead, I put two and two together while I was walking. I knew who the white man since he was a legend in Chitina.

What I had seen wasn't too complex. It was surprising, but when I put it with what I already knew, it wasn't hard to understand what had happened. Big Jake Severtsen and "Deefy" were dallying in her old cabin. Both of them were royally drunk.

"Deefy" was a pitiful looking person. She was toothless, little, and scrawny. I had seen her before, but never as the enthusiastic gymnast, who had somersaulted down the hill. That had to have been the happiest, most expressive thing I had ever seen anybody do in my life! As the only available, single woman in a town of 75 people, and supposedly being deaf and dumb, I don't know how she survived. And I would never know any of that, or how her life continued afterward. What a contrast there was between Big Jake and "Deefy". Yet these two people apparently shared a basic earthiness with one another. Most of the people I knew in Chitina would have thought it unbelievable that the two of them would have been together.

Big Jake was very well regarded and admired by the white community. He was always grandly welcomed to Chitina and his company was relished by everyone. He usually came to town at the end of each of his trapping runs. This time he had come to town just to buy supplies. It was too early to trap. Before the river froze and the cold came, he would run repetitive trips down the full length of the Chitina River to the Copper River at Chitina, working a trapline. Each trip would take ten days and he would stay for a short while in

24

Chitina before having my dad fly him back
upriver. He used a foldaboat or a folding
canoe for the 80-mile downriver trapping run.
He worked by himself, and he was always
successful.

Big Jake Severtsen was a very competent
man. It seemed he could do almost anything. He
was a guide, a trapper, a mountain climber, a
recluse, a hunter, and a charmer. He was a big
man with a good reputation for getting things
done in the back country. To me, he was another
one of an endless parade of unique people who
appeared in Chitina when I was there in the late
1940's.

The day after I saw Big Jake and "Deefy"
together, I overheard my mother chatting with
someone about Big Jake and her conversation
brought him into focus. She said that he was
cordial and well-regarded and welcome anywhere.
His origin was unknown. He lived in the back
country of the Chitina River because he hated
civilization. Three or four days was the most he
could tolerate staying in town. The last part
of each sojourn was always accompanied by heavy
drinking. Jake was a true escapist.
For whatever reason, on that early, foggy
morning, I was granted a quick look at two
people who were beyond our usual world. The
memory of "Deefy" tumbling down the hill still
astonishes me. There seemed to be tenderness,
happiness, and an escape from reality for both
parties concerned.

It was a rare moment!

Several years later, I couldn't believe my
eyes as I watched a film in which Big Jake
appeared. I was in the gym of the University of
Alaska, when the film was shown on a Sunday
night. Several students showed a film about a
mountain cliimbing expedition, which they had
made two summers before. There was a sequence
showing the university group meeting Big Jake

and his two companions. One was Mr. Reid, a Chicago restaurteur, and the other was a Swiss mountaineer. Wealthy, Mr. Reid had been in the first party to climb Mt. Logan in 1925, and he had returned to climb it again.

Jake Severtsen kicked a stream into submission with just his shoe-pac clad feet. He made a fast-running mountain stream become a near-dry crossing high on the slopes of Mt. Logan.

Let me explain what Jake did to that stream. He literally kicked the heck out of it, moving about a ton of gray, stream rock, diverting the main course of the stream and doing it in front of at least six witnesses, one of whom had a movie camera. I never learned from the student climbers if the stream was tough to cross, why they didn't cross it somewhere else, or why "Big Jake" was the only one moving the stream rock. He looked as if he had gone berserk as he made a place for the men to cross the stream there.

I think he was probably doing something necessary, but I also think he was showing off and doing it only because no else who was there could do what he was doing. It was terrific to see! It reminded me of a grizzly bear digging great gobs of dirt, while going after a ground squirrel.

Although the student climbers never explained what happened to the Reid party and Big Jake, I know that all the students completed their climb except for Harvey Turner, who had to stop because of altitude sickness.

I wouldn't have been surprised if the film had shown Big Jake carrying Mr. Reid and his Swiss aide up and down the mountain on his back. That Chitina fellow certainly had the strength to do just that!

# COPPER RIVER

Anyone living on a watercourse, large enough to be called a river, knows how important it is. Each person's life can be affected by the water and the local inhabitants are probably aware of the river's moods, its seasonal differences and the facts which describe it. In addition, there can be myths which give an interesting spirit to a river.

The town of Chitina has two rivers, the Copper and the Chitina. Both are full-bodied, treacherous, unpredictable, and overwhelming. During their brief exposure to modern man, neither of these rivers has been touched or altered, let alone controlled. Until the late 1800's only a few explorations had been made by Russians as well as U. S. Army surveyors. At the turn of the century only one major development, the building of the Copper River and Northwestern Railway had occured. The 30-year life of the railroad showed these two rivers to the world. The Guggenheim interests of New York helped develop interior Alaska, but only as a spin-off of their main effort to mine copper at Kennicott. They did this by providing a quick and reliable means of transportation of supplies and people through Chitina from Cordova to McCarthy and Kennecott.

Mounds of supplies would be unloaded at Chitina and then trucked as far away as Fairbanks via the Edgerton Cutoff and the Richardson Highway. This route was well used until the United States built the Alaska Railroad from Seward to Fairbanks in 1916.

The C. R. & N. W. R. W. was affected by the river in the most obvious way. The river was not only the guideline for a grade-level railroad, but it was its major obstacle to building it as well.

Consider the logistical problems the builders faced. First, there just wasn't a long, flat ribbon of land along the banks of the river on which to build a roadbed. Steep canyon walls plunged straight down into the river and required extensive hard-rock dynamiting to carve out miles of roadbed. After this was accomplished, it soon became apparent that much of the run along the steep canyon walls needed snowsheds which would project over the track to ward off avalanches of snow during the winter.

Second, the river is fed by countless streams, small rivers and glaciers. Each stream had a canyon or a ravine which had to be spanned with a wooden trestle made from giant trees. To get them, they had to be shipped to Cordova by sea from thousands of miles away because the local trees were too small for the task. They had to build over 26 miles of bridges along the 196-mile railroad!

Third, the seasonal snowmelt and ice breakup of the rivers required special consideration to insure that an adequate road elevation would be built to avoid flooding and washouts. The bridge, which crossed the Copper River at Chitina to connect the railroad to the remaining 65 miles running parallel to the Chitina River along its north bank, washed out every year at spring breakup. A permanent bridge was finally built across the river in the early 1970's, many years after the railroad had shut down. But during the life of the railroad, the quarter mile span between the supports on the west and east banks of the Copper River was replaced each spring by a brand-new, wooden trestle bridge.

The ice would take out the old bridge and the bridge builders would install a new one in less than two weeks. The railroad people bragged that the replacement cost of the bridge each year was only $37,000! A replacement was so cheap that a permanent bridge was never built at Chitina by the railroad.

Fourth, the impact and positioning of the glaciers, which emptied into the Copper River, forced the building of a magnificent steel bridge between the two great riverine glaciers, known as Miles and Childs. with the bridge quartering northward upstream. The permanent bridge, which was built between them, was far advanced for its time. It was constructed for a very special purpose in unusual conditions. It cost more than one million dollars to build, and from the date of its completion until now it has always been known as The Million Dollar Bridge. Regretably, it is unsafe to use today because a major support on one end of it slumped as the result of the 1964 earthquake. The epicenter of the quake was in Prince William Sound near Valdez, only 50 miles to the west.

It was along this area of unforgiving glaciers that the roadbed had to be built on land which moved. The terminal moraines of several glaciers lay in the path of this "Iron Trail". This section of the route required extra care and its track had to be relaid each year. One year after the railroad closed in 1938, this part of the railroad became impassable.

After the railroad was built the river was never used as a freight carrier. There was no economic need for doing so because the railroad handled all the freight. However boats were not strangers to the river. There were at least three steamboats used during the construction of the railroad. After the steel rails were in place, one of the steamboats was dismantled and rebuilt into a modest, two-story frame house in Chitina.

The Indians living in the Chitina area were known as the Ahtna. They traveled the river in winter when it became a river of ice

31

and snow.  No boats, no canoes were necessary
for them to move from one place to another.
Thus the local Indians were not river travelers
in the usual sense.  The surveyors, who preceded
the construction of the railroad, used canoes,
hugging the shores which gave them an upstream
push from an eddying action along the banks of
the river.  The famed Otto A. Nelson, a former
Deputy U. S. Commissioner and later U. S.
Postmaster of Chitina, during the 1940's and
1950's, first came to Chitina in a canoe as a
railroad surveyor.

Today, there are foldaboats, zodiac rafts,
and high-powered salmon guide boats made of
stainless steel and aluminum, with jetted
engines plying the river.  They travel all over,
fishing for salmon, and promoting whitewater
adventures.

A day in the life of the Copper River in
the summertime goes something like this:
Morning calm, little air movement, no dust in
the air.  However, if the sun is shining, all
that changes.  As the land heats, the
temperature difference between the land and
water produces an increasingly fierce wind which
races downriver, carrying tons of fine river
silt in the air.  It pushes this fine dust into
every house, into everyone's clothes, hair,
eyes, and ears.  The silt gets into everything!

Winter is different, of course.  No dust.
No air movement.  It brings a deep cold to the
land, locking the river in its icy grip.  The
frigid cold of winter lays one common
temperature over river and land alike.  During
the winter of 1949, my dad, Hildreth "Pappy"
Steelman, drove a Caterpillar tractor across the
river and brought back an old railroad bus from
the other side.  O.A. Nelson planned to
convert it back to its normal configuration as
a regular bus.  Pappy said that the combined
weight of the two big pieces of equipment made

a traveling depression so deep in the ice that it was like driving in the bottom of a trough. He reasoned that the trip was perfectly safe because the ice was several feet thick, nevertheless it was still an unnerving experience for him.

Even in the depths of the coldest time of winter, the river continues to flow along its bed, well beneath the heavy layer of frozen ice on the surface. The water is clear, not the gray-brown, silt-laden flow seen during the summer. For a ghostly experience, a person might walk out on the ice of the frozen river at night, during the dead of winter, under a bright moon and a starlit sky. And then just stand there and listen. Just listen! Cracking, popping noises punctuate the rushing of the deep, running river. It looks like an unmoving, solid-white frozen mass of ice. But in reality, the river is still very much alive, only its movement is down deep, out of sight. The combination of snow, moonlight, starlight, the hard cold, and the strange sounds coming from the frozen river create a unique and unforgettable experience.

Our government controls the Copper River today. This control has grown in proportion to the economic importance of salmon as a renewable resource. Permits are now required to dipnet salmon at Chitina and are granted yearly with daily quotas. During the salmon runs, people drive to Chitina by the hundreds from all over Alaska to catch red, silver, and king salmon in dipnets of all sizes and makes.

Today's high-tech sport nets are far different than the dipnets we used when I was a kid. In the late 1940's, we used a heavy, chicken-wire basket fastened to an iron circle strapped to a long, heavy, very stout wooden pole. This is a far cry from the nylon nets and lightweight metal poles used today.

We used to walk down a trail along the river-
bank to a place called The Point.  It was a
gravel finger jutting far out into the river.
Three or four old, heavy nets were left lying on
the ground for anyone to use.  A person dipped
the basket into the water, where it disappeared
under the surface of the gray silty flow, and
pointed the mouth of the net downstream into the
eddies which curled upstream.  The salmon hugged
the shoreline, taking advantage of the upstream
push the eddies gave them. The fisherman just
waited until he felt a bump and movement in the
net.  He couldn't see anything, but he felt the
action of the salmon caught in the chickenwire
net, bumping and trying to swim upstream.

I doubt if anyone walks out to The Point
today or even fishes there.  I went to Chitina a
few years ago and watched in horror at the
people dipping for salmon. They drove their
pickup trucks off the road, across sandbars and
the shallow, braided streams which appear along
the bend of the river at low water.  Then they
stood chest deep in the turgid, silt-laden water
pulling their nets back and forth through in
front of them.  While I was watching, I saw one
truck try driving across a small stream only to
have its back wheels silt over in seconds,
making it immovable.  A little later, I saw a
man upended by the fast current, his waders
sticking straight up in the air.  Someone
grabbed him and pulled him to safety.  There
were about 25 people fishing in the area, all
fighting for good positions and none of them
seemed to appreciate the danger of the swift
river.

In the '40's, we would never have stepped
into the river, let alone stand chest deep in
it.  The railroad documented 28 drownings in
the river while it operated, but it only
recovered the bodies of two men who drowned.
The other 26 had immediately silted down and

were lost forever.  The two bodies, which were
recovered, were of an engineer and a fireman who
were pulled out of the cab of a locomotive which
had fallen into the river.  If the men hadn't
been in the cab, their bodies would have been
lost forever too.  Thus  you can imagine my
astonishment at seeing all those darn fools
dipnet fishing in the new and careless way!

The old people, the Ahtna Indians, traded
with the Eyak Indians in the winter, walking the
length of the Copper River south to the delta
area.  They traded their handiwork, skins,
hides, copper tools and nuggets mainly for
candlefish oil carried in watertight spruce
boxes.  This oil was the main reason for their
trading.  The Copper River was their highway
long ago.  A grade-level, white snow and ice
trade route.  It ran right down the middle of
the frozen river, giving the Ahtna a hard road
on which to travel.

Early communications between the Ahtna and
Eyak Indians brought information regarding the
time of year for both tribes to meet in order to
trade.  Perhaps they traveled when the moon rose
at a certain time.  Through the millennia, this
trading was beneficial to each Indian group.  It
was unlikely that warring occurred between them,
because that would have hindered their trade.
Marriages probably happened but such information
hasn't been documented.  The Eyaks are too
closely aligned with the Ahtna through years of
trading not to have had alliances occur.  A
trading party was unlikely to have had a woman
along, as women generally remained at home in
the traditional sense, caring for the young,
keeping the home fires burning, and nurturing
the family while the men hunted, traded, and
wandered afar.

It is common today to couple running water
with hydroelectric power because we know
that water running downhill produces

electricity. The great dams in our West brought relatively cheap and inexhaustible power to our cities, farms, and industries. So it is a familiar concept to contemplate. There is a natural dam site just below the town of Chitina near the ancient village of Taral. The Copper River becomes giant-sized after absorbing the Chitina River and then narrows into a gorge cut through Woods Canyon, a granite opening.

Had the Kennecott Copper Mine and its attendant railroad stayed open past 1938, the advent of World War II might have caused our government to seek copper production and most probably would have advanced it well beyond its highest production levels. It is only logical to believe that this could have happened. The coastal shipping lanes would have been well protected because copper would have been a high-priority metal for the war effort, and most likely for the next several years there would have been a huge amount of government-inspired development in the Cordova-Chitina-McCarthy areas. Other minerals might have been mined there and shipped also.

Would a hydroelectric dam been built too? Maybe not. But the site is still there and boundless mineral wealth remains in the Wrangell Mountains. All that mining potential might have been too enticing for the wartime developers to ignore.

In contrast, there was a little hydroelectric power plant in Chitina in the 1940's and 1950's when I was there. O. A. Nelson and his son, Adrian, built a D. C. (direct current) power plant just below the old railroad bed at the edge of the river. They supplied its water from a penstock sited high on the side of the mountain at the west of town. They didn't use the water from the river to run the power plant. They used fresh, unsilted water so as not to damage the blades

of the power plant turbine. The spent water
spilled into the river. The accelerated fall of
water from the penstock was more than enough to
run the plant. Everybody's house in Chitina was
wired into the system though the Indian village
wasn't connected to it. Electricity was free
for those who were hooked up to the system. The
outflow from the powerhouse had to be screened
in order to keep the salmon from swimming into
its piping.

Although the Indian village, just south of
the Chitina townsite, was partially absorbed
into the white culture, it was horribly impacted
by the gangs of white people who built and
worked on the railroad and the mine. In spite
of that impact, the village men still trekked
far and wide in the winter, trapping and hunting
as they had always done, along the great rivers.

The double-sized Copper River, twice as
big after the Chitina River joins it, rushes
south to the Gulf of Alaska as a massive, gray-
brown crashing entity. It feeds one of the
largest and widest river deltas in the northland
of Alaska. The Copper River Delta is over 50
miles  wide and  stretches from Point Whiteshed
on its west end, near Cordova, all the way to
Katalla in the east, a great lowland braided
with  countless streams and waterways, all
working  their way to the Gulf of Alaska. The
moderate temperature of this seacoast world and
comparative safety of its marshes, willows,.and
trackless  sands  makes the delta a safe, almost
predator-free  stopover  for  the
largest assemblage of migratory waterfowl along
the Pacific Coast. The Copper River drainage
is filled with life, but nowhere is it more are
magnificent in its effect than in the Copper
River Delta.

There is a good reason to write about the
Copper River and the Chitina River as if they
were just one river. At their junction, the

Chitina River is the larger of the two rivers, but the geological formation casts the major dominance to the Copper River and its course. The suffix *na* as seen in the word Chitina means river in the Ahtna language. The word for copper in Ahtna is *chiti*. Therefore, the Copper River River flows into the Copper River at the Copper River! The Chitina River flows into the Copper River at Chitina.

Although today, the TransAlaska Pipeline parallels the Copper River for several miles and the townsites of Chitina, Copper Center, and Gulkana continue as settlements, the structure of the lands below Chitina and the establishment of the vast, federal Wrangell-St. Elias Preserve keep the river system and its drainage much the same as it has always been. However there have been some inroads.

When Walter Hickel was governor of Alaska the second time, he attempted to build a Copper River Highway down the river towards the coast from Chitina. He was stopped by a host of organizations, including the Chitina Village Corporation, Ahtna, its parent native corporation, various environmental groups, as well as public opinion. Mr. Hickel was having the Department of Transportation bulldoze a pioneer road down the old railroad right-of-way without securing permits or without considering the impact on any archeological sites of the natives along the route.

Regardless, the Copper River continues to flow southward to the Gulf of Alaska as it always has. Unimpeded and unbridled, its bordering glaciers and mountains rim the mighty watercourse as it rushes into its huge delta to welcome the millions of salmon and thousands of marveling visitors who come to see this area each year.

# PETE PENOFF

My mother took me over to Pete Penoff's cabin late one winter afternoon when I was home for Christmas from school in Cordova. She had baked a fruitcake for him as a token Christmas present.

I had never met Mr. Penoff, but from that one visit I have never forgotten him. You'll see the reason for this.

He was an older man in his mid-sixties and slightly built. His black hair was streaked with gray on the sides, and he had a rapid-fire way of speaking. Mr Penoff had an accent, of course! He was a Russian.

When we went inside his place, we could hardly breath it was so hot! I mean real hot! The temperature was easily in the mid-90's. Hot rooms in the middle of December in Chitina were usually a wonderful pleasure to enjoy because Chitina winters were so cold! The weather and temperatures rivaled those of Fairbanks and it was, at most, 30 below zero that day.

But Mr. Penoff's place wasn't wonderful after all!

True, it was hot and we probably would have gotten used to that heat and enjoyed it, except for one other thing. Pete Penoff loved garlic. He smelled of garlic. In fact he reeked of it! He carried a bunch of garlic cloves in his shirt pocket and he constantly nibbled on them. Along with the heat of the superhot cabin, the invisible cloud of garlic odor was overpowering!

It seemed as if we stayed there forever, visiting Mr. Penoff. But we finally left! When we stepped outside into that frigid and marvelously clear winter night, all those years

39

ago, nothing in the world smelled sweeter
than that fresh blast of crisp, arctic air!
And, thinking about it now, nothing has ever
smelled quite as sweet since.

# O'BRIEN CREEK

The first trestle bridge south of Chitina, along the old railroad right-of-way, crossed a fast-running, grayling stream called O'Brien Creek. It was located in a beautiful setting. From the high bank on the north, where the bridge pointed south, one could see the tremendous flow of the Copper River as it rushed through Woods Canyon with the Hanagita Range towering behind it. To the right was that lonely spire of native mystery, Spirit Mountain, due south of O'Brien Creek. The creek itself sprang out of a deep canyon on the right to the west, flowed under the trestle bridge, and then poured into the river about a hundred yards farther downstream. The trestle measured a good 100 yards across and 80 feet above the three-part stream below. The stream ran swiftly in its main channel against the south bank, with two smaller channels spurting down the middle of the creek bottom.

The best fishing prospects seemed to be in the main channel on the other side of the creek and, of course, there were only two ways to get over to that side. One was to cross the trestle bridge. The other was to climb down the near bank and then ford the two smaller channels of the creek.

The lure of getting across to the other side, to fish from the far bank, was impossible to satisfy from using a wading approach. The water was too deep. It appeared that the best way to get over to the other side was to cross the trestle.

And so, back in the summer of 1948, 10 years after the railroad had shut down, there was one venturesome 15-year-old boy with a hand-me-down fly rod getting ready to get across O'Brien Creek by climbing on its old wooden trestle bridge.

It looked all right. All he had to do was walk down the middle of the bridge and not get too excited about how high above the water he was because it was a long way down.

Although he was alone, he was actually relieved to be walking on the trestle. The trek down the old railroad track from Chitina was kinda scary. The right-of-way had deteriorated into a trail going through a growth of new alders. The ties and rails had long since been pulled up and taken away so the walking was easy. But the closeness of the surrounding alders and berry bushes seemed to be hiding bears all along the way. The fact that he hadn't seen any bear sign or tracks, and that there were a couple of unsprung rabbit snares set by the native kids, had done little to reassure him that he was safe from the monsters. No, the trestle was both a quick way to get across the wide stream bed and a haven of relief after his nervous walk.

The old trestle wasn't a footbridge. The only difference between it and a regular railroad installation, with ties on the ground, was that there wasn't any ground showing between the ties on the trestle. There was only air and if you looked straight down it seemed a lot farther down than only 80 feet!

It would have taken him four minutes at most to cross the bridge and climb down to fish on the other side. But right at the middle of the bridge, exactly right at its halfway point, where it's just as far to go one way as it is to go the other, the ties disappeared.

He stopped short.

What to do now? The rails hadn't been stripped from the bridge. They still stretched across the gap where the ties had been. There just weren't any ties to walk on.

Instead, there was a huge gap!

44

Although that imposing space was only
eight feet across, it looked wider than the
Grand Canyon!

In the ten years since the railroad had
shut down, a severe case of undercutting by the
middle fork of the stream below had occurred.
The main pair of pilings were still embedded in
the ground, but now they were tipped away from
vertical by about ten degrees. The cross
members connecting the vertical pilings on top
had been sheared off and the capping ties had
fallen down to the creek bed below. Only the
two steel rails were left suspended in midair.
So, the two ways to get across the creek were to
go back, climb down the bank, then try to wade
across as far as possible and still not get  to
the  good  main stream, or cross the bridge by
jumping the eight-foot gap. Well, he reasoned,
you can only stand there just so long and nerve
and unnerve yourself just so much. Besides you
know you can do a running broad jump of almost
18 feet.

The jump was clean, taking off from the
last tie, with just a little bobble on landing.
But it was a good jump. Elated, the boy never
looked back and quickly ran across the trestle
and climbed down the far bank to the good
fishing.

Not every cast raised a strike, but every
place that picketed the rushing water into a
feeding hole had a grayling in it. They would
come straight up and bite his black gnat fly and
pull it down under water with a sharp tug and
jerk. Their small mouths loved the black gnat.

One  grayling  was big, and, oh!, so
beautiful! It was iridescent and shiny with
black spots spread along its three-inch dorsal
fin. Maybe it weighed two pounds. It was
the biggest grayling he had ever caught.

And then, too soon, it was time to leave.
It  was  midafternoon  and he had to get back

home. He had work to do so it was time to
leave. And, of course, he now had to backtrack
the way he had come, up the bank and across the
trestle. There was no other way across the
main stream that he could see. He had wanted to
go back across the valley floor, maybe even by
walking along one of the stringers fastened near
the bottom of the giant timbers, but they were
too high to reach, especially when he was
carrying something. Each stringer stretched 20
feet from piling to piling, so he decided to go
back the way he had come.

He climbed to the top of the trestle with
its eight-foot gap he would have to jump. But
this time it would be different. This jump
wouldn't be the same as the one in the morning.
First, he was going to have to jump it going in
the opposite direction. Second, the afternoon
warming had caused the wind to pick up, and it
was blowing at right angles to the direction of
the jump. Third, he now had an armload of fish
to carry. Fourth, and probably most important,
he had too much time to think about what he had
to do!

Again, the take-off was good, but this
time, while in midair, the fish slapped against
his leg and, in reflexively adjusting for this
movement, his right hand opened just enough to
let his fly rod slip away to float down to the
valley floor, far below. It was gone! He
crouched and turned as he landed. The wind
seemed to be blowing even harder. He looked
down for his pole. It was really gone. In
fact, it was nowhere to be seen. The deepest
arm of the creek was directly below him. The
pretty, little fly rod had disappeared into
O'Brien Creek.

He felt really sad! He had enjoyed the
day so much. He had caught such a beautiful
grayling! He had felt the exhilaration of
crossing the trestle. And now this had

46

happened!

But there would be other fly rods, other disappointments and obstacles to overcome, as well as triumphs. But the breath-catching moment of that day long ago never left the boy and, as a man, much later, its memory helped shape his perspective and his appreciation of how wonderful life could really be.

# KLAUS

I've told this story many times, often in the hope that I could remember the last name of the man I was talking about. Maybe it was Naske. I don't think so, but let's use that name anyway. Klaus Naske.

Many oldtimers stayed in Chitina in the winter. Most construction jobs were seasonal in Alaska during the 1940's. The high-tech systems, which we take for granted today weren't in place yet. The country was just getting over World War II, and times in Alaska during the winter were quite slow-paced. Chitina was a good place to get away from it all. Rural Alaska had its share of trappers, prospectors, remittance men, government people, equipment operators, adventurers, climbers, and lots of ordinary folks, such as truckers, bush pilots, storekeepers, lodge owners, bullcooks, bartenders, commercial fishermen, people involved in small-town things, kids and natives. Most of the oldtimers in Chitina were bachelors in their sixties and seventies, who had been all around the territory, doing all kinds of things, working when they needed to, hunting, fishing, and hibernating in the winter.

Chitina was a long way from most other places. It was a good place to hole up. No one ever asked nosy questions. People were accepted at face value. I only wish I knew more about the six to ten older men who lived in the town in the winter staying in their small cabins. But stories about them from my folks gave me some insight into their lives. The fellow whose story this is about was a man named Klaus and his last days were spent in a blaze of surprise to the other residents of Chitina.

48

My folks had known Klaus for most of the
two plus years they lived in Chitina. However,
he was a casual acquaintance. I think he had
stopped by their place a few times and may have
even been a guest for dinner. But the last
time he showed up in the middle of winter was
different. He was practically incoherent. Mom
thought he was drunk by the way he was talking
and acting, but he wasn't. He didn't take a
drink when one was offered and soon left. Not
long afterward, my folks heard a sharp crack
which prompted them to go outside. They found
Klaus lying in their driveway back near the
small barn behind the house where they kept
their old Dodge panel truck.

They got Klaus to his feet and headed him
toward his own place. He didn't speak to them
at all and seemed totally spent. He died a
couple of days later.

The big, double doors to the garage barn
were wide open in front of the place where
Klaus was found lying on the ground. To keep
the doors shut, a two-by-six cross bar
swivelled on the inside of the doors into two
metal keepers. You couldn't open these doors
from the outside. But Klaus had opened that
door, snapping the cross piece in two, before he
had collapsed. There was a personnel door on
the side of the garage barn which one
normally went into to get to the truck. The
crossbar would have had to have been lifted
from the inside to open the big doors.

The medical report revealed Klaus' cause
of death and showed what probably allowed him to
perform this superhuman feat of strength. Klaus
was irreversibly ill from syphilis which had
reached its final and deadly third stage. He
had tertiary syphilis. For some unknown reason,
he had wanted to open the garage door, had
grabbed the outside of the two big doors
and, with his body and mind off kilter, had an

adrenalin surge, which allowed him to snap the doors open! It had apparently taken all of his energy and he had collapsed on the spot.

No, he hadn't gone into the garage and pushed the doors open from inside, snapping the crossbar that way. No one had gone through the regular door at all. There was fresh snow on the ground and there weren't any tracks leading to the door, just Klaus' footprints going to the big double doors.

Can you imagine living with syphilis all those years. He had to have known he had it. What a terrible way for him to die!

# CHASE AND THE CHITINA CASH STORE

Nobody ever ran a store like Chase did!
You've probably all heard about one-man country
stores, but there is no way you could call the
Chitina Cash Store an ordinary country store or
its keeper, Melvin Chase, an ordinary country
store-keeper. Chase was a fixture at the Cash
Store where he had been working for O. A.
Nelson, doing everything the place demanded for
many years. It was the last stop for hundreds
of miles in every direction, where a person
could get almost anything worth buying.

O. A. Nelson owned Chitina in 1949. He
had kept it alive after the Kennecott Copper
Mine and its Copper River and Northwestern
Railway closed down in 1938. As mentioned
before, O. A. had been a territorial Deputy
Commissioner, was the U. S. Postmaster, and had
bought the platted townsite of Chitina from the
railroad when it shut down. If O. A. Nelson was
the king of Chitina then Melvin Chase was its
prince.

Not a prince charming by any stretch of
the imagination, just the prince in charge of
running the castle. The castle was The Chitina
Cash Store. Describing the store described
Chase.

The store was a sprawling, old, ram-
shackle, one-story frame building with its large
main store up front. Behind that great room, on
one side, was a good-sized storeroom, a large
freezer room, and Chase's quarters in back on
the other side. Chitina had electric power from
the riverside power plant which O.A. and his son
had built so there was electricity for the
freezer and a few bare light bulbs which didn't
quite cut the gloom inside the hulking old
store.

Shelving ringed all the walls of the main

room with several aisle stacks along the middle
of the floor. This emporium sported all kinds
of treasures from canned goods and sacks of
flour and sugar to a mixed assortment of
clothes and dry goods. In the exact center of
the main room stood a double-barreled wood
stove, which gobbled up at least a quarter cord
of wood a day during the frigid winter months.
It was generally believed that The Chitina Cash
Store had everything. A customer just had to be
able to find it. And for the hundreds of souls
from miles around, this assertion was taken as
gospel.

Chase stocked most everything one might
need in 1940 rural Alaska, from tobaccos and
pearl oil to cold storage eggs and sides of
beef. It was all there, except stamps, fishing
lures, flies, and curios which O. A. sold
separately across the street in the post
office. That two-story, log building sat
cattycorner from The Cash Store.

Presiding over this eclectic retail world
was Melvin Chase. A man in his late fifties
with a large torso, always seen wearing dark-
brown clothes, head topped with an ever-present
gray fedora, a cigarette glued to his lower
lip. He always had a twinkle in his blue eyes.
He acted grumpy but beneath his scratchy
exterior was a real nice person. Chase did all
the work at the store. Once in a while though
O. A. would help out, but Chase usually did
everything himself. He ordered supplies,
received them, stocked them, priced everything,
prepared, butchered, sold, and bundled items for
reshipment. He did it all.

Most of the items in the store arrived
from Seattle via the Alaska Steamship Company
and then carried the last 131 miles overland to
Chitina by Roy McCrary in his stake-bed truck.
In the late 1940's, Thompson Pass, 20 plus miles
out of Valdez, was closed to winter

traffic so most of the Cash Store's supplies had
to be received during the summer and fall.

I don't know where Chase came from.
O. A. Nelson came from Keokuk, Iowa, and I think
that Chase might have come from the Midwest
too. When we knew him, he had been a bachelor
all his life, but after we moved away from
Chitina in 1950, O. A.'s widowed sister, Mabel
Lyon, came back to town and the last we heard,
she and Chase had married and moved to
California. O. A. hired other men afterward to
run his store, but after 20 plus years as
Chase's place, the store just wasn't the same
anymore.

Random thoughts crowd into my mind about
Chase. As a bachelor, he loved a good meal,
especially if he didn't have to cook it, and
when my mother hosted an evening meal on a
regular basis for the few bachelors in Chitina,
during the winter, Chase seemed to be the most
appreciative diner who ate at our house. I
remember that he always called my mother,
"Missus".

He was really a nice man, just a little
grumpy at times. Once, when my folks left me in
charge of the old hotel which she and O. A. had
opened to handle the summer tourists, I ended up
running things for three days, while mom and
dad were up the Chitina River visiting Charley
Kramer's Chititu Mine. My job didn't entail
much work. It was during the middle of the week
so there were no guests. I just had firewood to
split, stoves to keep going, do general cleaning
and cook an evening meal for the same old
regulars my mother had cooked for during the
winter.

One of the dinners which mom had planned
for me to fix featured a small roast of beef.
It was real easy to prepare. I just had to
roast it in the oven. Then I only had to heat
some vegetables, make a salad, cut some pie,

make coffee, and mash enough potatoes for the four of us.

I knew that we should have gravy, but since I had never made gravy before, I had a real hard time getting it to darken, so I reasoned that the more Kitchen Bouquet I used, the darker it would get. It didn't turn out the way I wanted it to. The gravy <u>looked</u> great, but it was terribly bitter!

The old regulars ate the dinner with relish, complimenting me all the while, never saying a word about my gravy. After mom came home, she asked me how I had made the gravy, and when I told her she broke down, laughing, until she saw how embarrassed I was, and stopped. Then she told me that the regulars, and specifically Chase, had mentioned the dinner and the gravy. Not one of those fine men ever said a word about my special gravy to me. They were all really kind. Many years have passed since then, but I have never forgotten their silent thoughtfulness.

The Chitina Cash Store was an institution and so was Melvin Chase. People regularly drove hundreds of miles to Chitina every year in the fall to buy their winter supplies. Some of them drove all the way from Valdez, a round trip of 262 miles through the mountains, to buy their supplies in Chitina instead of buying them in Valdez. It was cheaper to shop in Chitina in spite of everything having been shipped through Valdez!

It was the difference in overhead, or, putting it another way, the difference was Melvin Chase!

# FLYING HOME

Ice cold!  The sharp smell of strange fluids and exhausts flooded the cramped, banged-up cockpit of the old Stinson SM8A.  I will never forget that smell.  Later flying experiences made me realize that I was truly afraid to fly in that forbidding old monoplane. Its exposed, radial engine was fiercely loud, rackety, and unmuffled.  It was a long, long way from the near-silent jet service we take for granted today.  Since I was usually airsick when I was flying as a teenager, all the discomfort and disorientation fed my fear, and the resulting flight was torture.

Years later, after I had learned to fly in the army, I often thought back to those terrible flights I had to take between Cordova and Chitina, and how I would have loved to fly them all over again without being afraid or sick.  The cold and discomfort were minor annoyances compared to them.  In spite of my malaise, the trips were great adventures and were filled with magnificent sights.

We would take off from the snow-covered, gravel strip next to Lake Eyak at Cordova, fly east five miles across the lake, then another 20 miles on to Aleganik on the Copper River, where we would turn left, north, and head upriver for the last 100 miles to Chitina.

I remember random sights of that awesome river.  The Copper River was no placid, agrarian watercourse!  Its steep walls were ragged chunks of rocks crouched along both sides of that dirty, gray torrent of water. Snowsheds stretched their covers over the abandoned railroad track along the west bank to keep as much snow as possible from cascading onto the rails.

The sheer canyon walls beside the river

were shoved aside in several places by an array of glaciers and their moraines, and also by several precipitous, smaller, tributary creeks and rivers. In its northbound trek, the railroad track had been laid across these terminal moraines. Oldtimers told me that the ever-moving moraines skewed the track in less than a year after the Copper River and North-western Railway shut down in 1938.

It didn't help my composure that the daylight during those wintry trips was gray at best, and that the mountainsides disappeared upward into a layer of snow clouds. I truly cannot remember the sun ever shining during those winter trips up and down the river. The starkness of the route was stamped into my memory as white on black, white snow on black rock. The noise of the radial engine was overpowering and the pilot, usually my dad, and I could only talk by shouting. My stepdad must have dreaded carrying his airsick stepson through these ordeals, but, bless him, he never complained.

The flights took a little over an hour. We would land on the ice of One Mile Lake just a short way north of town. Mom and my sister, Mary-Linda, would often meet the plane and everything would then be as I had hoped. I was home again! Thanksgiving Vacation lasted for a week. Again, I flew during the Christmas holidays and then back to Cordova in early January for school. Summertime was different. It meant that I would be home in Chitina from the end of May until early September.

It was flying to Chitina in the winter, in beat-up, old airplanes smelling of hot oil and solvents, and gripped hard by the frigid cold which I remember more distinctly.

58

# THE GHOST TOWN GAZETTE

The following is copied from an issue of a mimeographed paper which O. A. Nelson printed in January, 1958, eight years after I graduated from high school. Some light might be shed on the workings of O. A.'s mind and his special brand of humor from reading this excerpt.

O. A. is obviously O. C., the Old Cynic, but I have no idea who Poncho is. A drawing in the paper shows O. C. as a ghost and Poncho as a sled dog. O. A. always liked to promote Chitina as a ghost town. When he and my mother reopened the old Commercial Hotel in 1948 they renamed it Spooks Nook.

---

## "THE GHOST TOWN GAZETTE"

The Old Cynic and Poncho will team up on this edition. If there is anything in it that you do not like, just blame it on either of us. That same pungent term is appropriate for either of us. Just smile when you use it. The recent heavy snows have driven the moose down from the higher hills where they have been living because here they are safer from the wolves. Jack Wilson who has been flying over the Chitina Valley on a wolf hunt says that moose are very, very numerous and wolves very scarce there, and that the light snowfall and the mild winter should mean that most of the moose will survive the winter. There will be some happy big game hunters in that area next fall. But the feed on the hills is short stuff and is now so deeply buried in the snow that it is impossible for the moose to get it. They are coming down into the valleys where there are taller willow, birch and poplar.

59

Robert Marshall said he saw sixteen moose in one stretch along the Valdez Road, and in spite of their long legs their bellies were dragging deep in the snow leaving a deep trough. They were making slow progress, but appeared to be fat and happy. If Doc Hoffman will send down a few of his protected wolves they can kill the whole herd in two hours, and they would. (No, that's not correct. The wolves kill only the old and weak). How goofy can some people get in their effort to get attention? Poncho is going to organize a society for the protection of mosquitoes and lampreys lest they become extinct. He nominates Doc Hoffman as first vice president in charge of feeding mosquitoes. What a monotonous country this would be without mosquitoes and wolves and mental cases to fill our mental health institutions.

---

If Al McCuen gets nominated and elected there will be at least two honest people in the next Legislature with aggressiveness and guts to take part in the next session of the legislature.

---

Paddy King traps south from town and Billy Buck traps out the road north. Each has gotten about a dozen lynx and Billy has trapped and shot several wolves on the east side of the Copper River. But Billy isn't a very good sport in this wolf game. He wears a white parka and the wolf thinks he is a ghost and as wolves are not afraid of ghosts he can walk right up to the wolf or the wolf to him. BANG! The poor wolf hasn't got a chance. Billy does

not exactly shoot from the hip but it is pretty
near that.

Several days ago Paddy shot at a wolf that
was standing sidewise to him. As usual he
was putting the bullet right into the wolf's
eye. But at the flash of the rifle the wolf
snapped at the bullet with his long jaws and the
bullet went right between his teeth. Then the
wolf turned tail and ran. Paddy pumped in
another shell and made a bull's eye.

---

Down among the clay hills of Missouri,
years and years ago, a homely spinster had a
lover. But the young man's interest in this
corn-fed Amazon faded, and she in frustration
and chagrin prosecuted him for rape. The Old
Cynic atended the trial so he could lilsten to
the testimony. The young defense attorney was
questioning her in the matter but was
embarrassed a bit and was fumbling badly. The
old judge broke in, "Madam, what he is driving
at is this. When this defendant, as you say,
was assaulting you, did you do all you could to
resist him and prevent the alleged rape?" And
the old gal replied, "Judge, I guess maybe I
should of resisted him, but it seemed so good Ah
jes couldn't".

We Alaskans who are for Statehood now know
that it does not make sense but the idea of a
handful of people having two senators in
Congress to trade votes for concessions for
Alaska is so alluring that we just can't resist
it.

---

IN KEOKOK, IOWA, a furniture store offers
a free set of Kinsey's volumes with each set of
bedroom furniture.

---

JUVENILE DELINQUENCY is proving that some parents just are not getting at the seat of the problem.

If you want to smoke cigarettes go ahead, no one is going to stop you. In fact those who make money out of the business will do all they can to encourage you. After all, you are going to die sometime soon anyhow. Cigarettes only make you die a bit sooner, and make you harder to live with before you die. But you'll have lots of fun!

We still question the sense and ethics of filling our best magazines with beautiful ads admonishing school girls to start smoking cigarettes. Anyone in Russia who did that would be shot or sent to Siberia. And too much liquor is bad. It makes you fight with your neighbor. It may even make you shoot at him, and it also may cause you to miss him.

---

There are no leaders unless there are willing followers. There are people all around who would very much like to be leaders but are not because they can inspire no following. Today the Russians willingly hand their resources over to their leaders because they believe these leaders are leading them to where they want to go.

"Follow me and we will conquer", promised Alexander, Julius Caesar, Napoleon, Stalin, Krushchev.

A leader is a man who senses which way the crowd wants to go and gets out in front and runs like hell. The Russian people are very proud of their scientists, planes, submarines, missiles and Sputniks and are willing to pay the price. Why do we Americans want to keep up the silly pretense that the Russian people are not willingly behind their leaders. It's not

nice to kid ourselves.  But then we Americans
bet on horse races even though we wonder if they
are fixed.

---

The Alaska Steamship Co. intended to
increase their rates by 15% last December but
recently announced that this increase has been
postponed for the present.  The competing
Coastwise Line has discontinued service to
Alaska in the meantime, and we hope that the
Alaska Line will have found that without sharing
the traffic to Alaska their revenues will be
sufficiently increased so that this rise in
rates will not be necessary.  One thing that we
who have done business with the Alaska Line for
about a half century can feel sure of is that an
organization that has over so many years built
up a reputation of being a vital part of Alaska
and of giving useful and generous service in
building the Territory has such pride in its
reputation that makes it an outfit that can be
counted on for honesty and fair treatment.

The behavior of the American economy
generally is typified by our local situation.
The place to cut firewood is on the other side
of the Copper River from town.  We have to sled
it across the ice after the river freezes in
late winter.  However, this winter thus far has
been so mild that the river has not frozen over
well and it looks doubtful if it will..  We are
wishing for a good, long cold spell that will
freeze the river so we can get over to cut some
wood that we would not need, if we did not burn
our present supply during this hoped for cold
spell.

---

The Old Cynic and Poncho find that they
are going to have to go down to Washington and
straighten out the mess that our country has

gotten into. Down in our capital the politicians seem to be overworked, trying to get satellites up, taxes down, and the other party out. They thought at first they would stop off at Juneau but decided that the situation there is one that cannot be improved. It is reported that down in Washington the stores are featuring hara-kiri knives.

---

Axle Bror Wahlstrom who is an oldtime miner, well into his seventies has lived here in Chitina for many years. In recent years he has been afflicted by arthritis. Recently, he got into such poor shape and helpless condition that he has gone to the hospital in Seward looking for relief. Axle is a small man but in his day he was a mighty man for work. In the good ole days, when drilling in the mining tunnels was all done by hand, Axle would take his ration of two candles and go to the face of the tunnel and get himself squared away on a hold and then blow out the candles to economize and whale away with the single jack for ten hours in the dark. Yes, those were the good old days some people think they want to come back.

---

The road into Chitina is in very good shape this winter. Very little snow and ice. The B. P. R. crew keeps it safe and it so winding that the drivers have to drive sane. No accidents or difficulties on this road. Anyone one living this side of Panama can drive right into Chitina if they are interested.

Vern and Nancy Newell who are living in the Lyons House, received word last week that Vern's father in Minnesota was very ill. They left hastily for Lake City but hope to be back soon.

64

It seems that Valdez has somewhat
overreached herself in building hospitals and
apartment buildings for which there is no
present need. But fortunately there have been
so many Alaskans that go squirrelly since
statehood phobia hit the Territory that now
Alaska is looking for places in which to store
its nuts. Some officials think these buildings
in Valdez could be very suitable.

The principal advantage advanced by the
people who want to keep our mentally ill people
here in Alaska is that doing this will bring a
payroll here. Also it is believed that the
mentally ill will be happier among old
acquaintances and people of their own kind who
understand them. Anchorage claims that the nuts
will find a more congenial companionship there
than in any other place in Alaska. Anchorage
seems to be winning this argument.

But don't bring these mentally ill people
to Chitina for nobody understands us anyway.

---

Only four months now and the trout will be
jumping two feet above the water at Tebay and
Hangita Lakes. However, we do not want anyone
to get a wrong impression about these trout.
When we say that the fish over there measure
about sixteen inches, we do not mean between the
ears as they do in Texas.

---

A few of our more energetic inhabitants
have been skating on the lake here recently.
Most years the snow is too deep.

---

An outstanding American exhibitionist who
writes under the captivating name of Norman

Vincent Peale answers a woman who writes to him wanting to know.

"How can I overcome the feeling that my husband is ugly?"

He gave this typical advice, "Always look for the best in people, even your own husband or wife."

Now isn't that just fine? We Indians agree that the white man needs more of those mental health delousers. If I had it to live over again, I think I would be a preacher.

---

Not long ago the Old Cynic got around to proposing to a young woman. He pointed out that he owned his own home, bed and cook stove and had some money in the bank. She said she would think it over. Next day she said, "No, I'll not marry you. You are only seventy three and look as if you are fairly healthy. Golly, you might live another ten years!"

---

Industrially, Alaska is a raw materials country or it is nothing. We can have no industry except those that are harvesting the natural resources. That has been true of all frontier countries. We may have gold mines, copper mines, mercury mines, hydro electric metallurgical-chemical plants, pulp plants, oil wells, fisheries, mental health plants and other industries based on our natural resources, but not in any foreseeable time will we do any considerable amount of manufacturing or farming. We just aren't that kind of country or people.

---

Old Cynic: "There are now twenty eight and a half people in this village, counting me".

Poncho: "Don't forget to count me, that makes it just twenty nine".

In a recent editorial of one of our leading newspapers, we notice this statement regarding the letters that are being written to various people in Washington and to newspapers. It sets out the writer's reasons for opposing statehood at this time.

"The results of this letterwriting campaign are gratifying. The letters are making no more splash than that of a feather wafted into a lake from the tail of a high-flying dove."

Then follows a garbled tirade against these letter writers who have just been dismissed as being inconsequential. Quite a splash for that tail feather.

The same editorial presumed to quote a majority of Alaskans by saying, "All Alaskans are not in favor of statehood". We think that statement is too sweeping and we believe most Alaskans would qualify the statement a bit and say "Nearly all Alaskans are not in favor of Statehood".

Really there must be quite a lot of Alaskans who are in favor of statehood now, though they are getting fewer all the time.

All of which reminds us of the mother who had three husky sons. When they grew up they went out West and started a ranch raising beef cattle. After they became quite prosperous they wrote back to their mother and asked her to suggest what she thought would be a suitable name for their ranch. She replied that she thought focus would be a very nice and appropriate name.

The boys wrote back saying they found the name focus to be very nice but they wondered why she thought it so very suitable.

She replied that focus means: "Where the Sun's rays meet".

Which story the rhetoricians call a spooneri parallelogram.

─────────────────────────────

The crocuses will be shoving up from the frozen ground and blooming among the snow patches the middle of April.


. . .and right there the page was torn. Many have been able to garner copies of other issues of O. A.'s paper through the years. This was the only one I had.

## RELIGION AND SALMON

Two white missionaries lived in the native
village.  Mr. and Mrs. Donahue were there to run
a school and to convince the Chitina Indians
that religion was necessary.  I never heard the
full story about them, about how long they had
lived there, or what their real impact was on
the community.  They lived and schooled in an
old gray building in the village.  No church
people are ever flush with money, and I'm sure
they were no exception.  They probably existed
on donations sent to them from afar.  But they
also made money by helping the villagers process
and can salmon which came from the fishwheels.

The village was dying by 1948.  There were
very few children, and fewer and fewer families
staying there because most of the more active
and skilled Indians had moved north to
Glennallen to work for the Road Commission,
operating graders and cats.  Those who were left
behind were barely surviving, either just above
or just below the poverty level of living.

I would have been surprised if the Indians
of Chitina had paid any attention at all to the
ministrations of the Donahues because the few
who were still there were a pretty  stoic  bunch
and never seemed very optimistic.  They didn't
appear to be a very receptive group for
missionary work.  There may have been church
services held then but, if so, they must have
been low keyed because none of the non-Indians,
with whom I came into daily contact, ever
participated in any services.  There was a small
church on the road to the village and even
though my family came from a strong Methodist
background, my folks never suggested going to
any service which might have
been conducted there.

But there was one splendid function which

the Donahues did promote and that was canning salmon. They taught the Indians, who had a surplus of salmon, how to can the fish in one-pound tall cans. The Donahues were able to control the process because they had the only steam cooker around which could handle a large volume of cans. Their huge pressure cooker could cook over a hundred cans at one time. Their processing, and the cut which they took, was probably what supported them. All they had to do was fire up a giant wood fire and cook the salmon provided by the natives and, consequently, none of the thousands of fish caught in the fishwheels ever went to waste.

But to get the fish to the canning table was a monstrous chore. It went something like this. The fishwheels were only allotted to Indian use when Alaska was a territory. No white person was allowed to operate a one. The wheels paddled unendingly day and night in selected spots along the west side of the Copper River, sometimes dumping an amazing horde of fish into their boxes. Big Susie King's wheel was located almost directly east of the village at the base of a 250-foot bluff and it was famous for catching more king salmon than any other fishwheel, up to 400 a day, during the peak salmon run! Big Susie, and whoever helped her, would gut and split the fish on the bank of the river and then hang them over racks of poles to air dry. After a couple of weeks she would load up a pack of the sun-dried fish and carry them up the zig-zag, sandy trail to the top of the bluff and then march to the village another half mile where she and Mrs. Donahue would cut the fish into can-sized pieces, pack the pieces into the cans, seal the cans, and then cook them. The few weeks of drying produced a kippered fish
and drastically reduced their weight, concent-rating its food value into a nutritious,

half-preserved chew, a salmon jerky. Full
processing of fish into salmon jerky would have
meant keeping the fish on the racks, air drying
them fully or enveloping the fish in an alder
smoke, which would give it a better flavor. But
there was only just so much room on the rocks
down by the river, and the fish kept coming, not
only from Big Susie's wheel, but from three or
four others, so the Donahues kept busy helping
the harvest of fish from May through September
each year.

The Donahues kept to themselves. I never
saw them at The Chitina Cash Store, but that
doesn't mean they didn't trade there. They were
in their middle 60's then. Mr. Donahue seemed
less able, less hardy, than Mrs. Donahue. She
seemed to work hard all the time. They probably
left the village before 1959 because when I made
it back to Chitina, after getting out of the
army, they were gone. The little old church
remained on the way to the village was there.
And they were still not holding any services
there, as far as I could see.

# O. A. NELSON

By today's measure, the bag of gold O. A. Nelson presented to the Seattle Bank of Commerce in 1958 for cash payment would have been worth well over five hundred thousand dollars. Back then, at $35 a fine ounce, his lifetime collection of dust and nuggets only amounted to a little over $54,000.

Today, over 40 years later and long-since dead, O. A. Nelson would have liked nothing better than to have befuddled the Seattle bankers with his half million dollars, His entrance into the bank in 1958 was front page news in the Seattle Post Intelligencer. The paper dedicated the bottom third of its front page to the story, sensationalizing the latter-day "gold king" from Alaska. For in the comparatively modern time of 1958 Seattle, it was unheard of for any Alaskan to sell gold to any Seattle bank, let alone for the grand amount of $54,000. Remember, this was during the time when an income of $10,000 was considered top pay in Alaska.

But that was O. A.! Not a grandstander in the conventional sense, who might have leapt up on a table and hollered out loud to get some attention, but a man whose actions and insight always demanded the attention he received.

I met O. A. Nelson when I was just turning 14. In 1947, I had flown from Cordova to Chitina to be with my folks on Thanks-giving. My parents had been transferred to this interior Alaska village so my dad could run Cordova Air Service's flying operation in the Copper River/Chitina River/Wrangell Mountain area, an area of over 25,000 square miles which included Chitina, McCarthy, Chestochina, and all points in between.

O. A. owned the Chitina townsite which he

73

had bought from the Copper River and Northwestern Railway when it abandoned its operation from Cordova to Kennicott in 1938. He was the U.S. Postmaster, had been a Deputy U.S. Commissioner, owned the drug store which housed the post office, and, most importantly, owned The Chitina Cash Store, the only general store for hundreds of miles. This store was the main supply provider to people living in the remote areas served by Cordova Air Service.

My first Thanksgiving in Alaska was celebrated with O. A. at his large apartment over the drug store. Counting my family, the Bill Camerons, the Hank Kvalviks, O. A. and Chase, there were a dozen for dinner.

O. A. was unprepossessing. He dressed the part of a working stiff, usually wearing a light, gray, striped workshirt and a pair of black breeches which he trimmed off above the ankles with a knife when his pant legs became too frayed. His pants were held up by a pair of yellow suspenders. He wore a pair of scuffed, brown work boots. To belie being just another, ordinary guy he always wore a trans-parent, green bookkeeper's visor, winter or summer.

So, at first sight, one saw a grubby, lean older man in somewhat tattered work clothes usually walking somewhere carrying a tool or a coil of rope, head bent over purposefully. Just another old sourdough.

But stop him in order to talk with him. See him face-to-face, and his true personality would enthrall you. His hair had turned white, he had wide set blue eyes, which were almost walleyed, thin lips, good teeth, and he was always clean shaven.

O. A. always had a project underway. The only times I remembered him not being on the go were at dinner. He had countless tasks to complete in his town. He not only had the Cash Store and the Post Office to take care of but

74

he also had all the old buildings and small
houses in the townsite. He had installed a
domestic hot-water system in the village which
served five places and he and his son, Adrian,
had built a direct-current (DC) power plant on
the bank of the Copper River which provided all
the electricity and power for his small
community.

His drugstore/post office housed a VHF
radio which linked my dad with Cordova and my
dad's boss, Merle Smith. There were always
visitors, travelers, trappers, government men,
as well as friends, who constantly stopped at O.
A.'s for a night's stay. Visitors usually
helped O. A. with his projects as mute payment
for his generous hospitality and for staying in
one of the bedrooms in his apartment.

O. A. Nelson and Chitina were synonymous.

For our family to have gone to Chitina
after its short, three-month stay in Cordova,
even coming from south New Jersey to Alaska, was
kind of like landing on the moon. My folks
lived in Chitina full time so they became
immersed in the place but I only went there for
Thanksgiving and Christmas vacations and the
summers. Mom put me to work helping her run an
old hotel she, my dad, and O.A. had opened for
the tourists. They renamed and outfitted the
old, rundown Commercial Hotel, calling it Spooks
Nook. The new name emphasized the ghost town
aspect of Chitina. Chitina in 1947 was remote,
rudimentary, frigid in the winter, and a dust
bowl in the summer when the afternoon winds came
up.

The town operated on a wood economy, petro
fuel being used to run cars and airplanes and to
light lanterns. Firewood meant having to fall
trees, buck them, transport them to town, and
then split them up. Splitting the
wood became a skill which I was forced to
develop as my mom's I had to keep three stoves

constantly going in the old hotel.

Remembering my airplane trips to Chitina
from Cordova, I flew there six times in the two
and a half years before my folks moved to
Palmer. Later on, two summers out of high
school, after finishing a construction job on
the Kenai, and on my way to college in
Fairbanks, I found I had an extra week before
school started, so I hitch-hiked over to Chitina
from Palmer. And, as so many before me, who
dropped in to visit O. A., I helped him with his
projects for those few days, digging ditches,
drilling holes to set points so he could
dynamite a huge earth slide which had broken the
water main which fed the power plant. O. A.
didn't even blink an eye when I showed up
unannounced on that early September night.
Reading his face from memory, my naive
appearance, a 19-year-old boy he hadn't seen in
two and a half years, didn't faze him one bit.
He just showed me where to sleep and let me help
him out. I stayed there four days and caught a
ride back to Palmer with some Fish and Game
guys.

O. A. enjoyed good conversation and, since
he was well read, his alertness and grasp of the
affairs of the territory and the nation meant
that he was also well versed on countless other
subjects. When he found out which side of an
argument someone favored, he would take the
other side of the issue and try to talk the
person to a standstill. He usually won these
verbal jousts. He may have been a surveyor from
Keokuk, Iowa, who came to Chitina in a canoe for
the railroad, but he was smarter and more
cosmopolitan than most of the people who lived
in the more civilized parts of any U. S. city.
His sense of humor was a precious gift which
usually showed after he decided to make
something happen. His idea of turning Chitina
into a ghost town was evidenced when he painted

large, white ghosts on the old garages and barns
in town.  During World War II, he pro-tected
Chitina by mounting a cannon above the town to
the east, high up on the hill between the town
and the river.  Anyone climbing up that hill
discovered that the cannon was a huge log
resting between two old wagon wheels.

Later on, his publication of the Ghost
Town Gazette would provide more insight and
humor to the "idjits" of our world.

The last time I saw O. A. was in 1961,
after he had suffered a stroke.  He was
recovering from its paralysis.  I went over to
visit him in one of the small houses he owned,
where he was living with, his new wife.  He
would have been 78 or 80 then.  He easily
remembered me, seemed pleased to talk, and heard
the news of my family.  He had been especially
fond of my kid sister, Mary-Linda, who had been
killed in an auto accident five years earlier.
It was hard for me to see such a vital man so
impaired.  And, although he talked haltingly and
couldn't move well, there was nothing wrong with
his still agile mind.

I recently met Sy Neeley of Glennallen at
a convention.  Sy shared an episode about O. A.
with me.  It seems that his parents arranged to
buy the old Chestochina store in the early
1940's from a Mr. Rowland.  The Neeleys only had
$3,000 to spend.  Mr. Rowland said he would take
$1,500 down and the balance in instalment
payments.  Repairing and putting the old  place
in order used up most of the balance of their
funds.  And at this point they still needed to
buy foodstuffs for resale in their store.

Someone suggested that they contact O. A.
Nelson in Chitina, that he might sell them their
needed items from his Cash Store.  So Mr. Neeley
went to see O. A. in Chitina, over a
hundred miles away.  Mr. Neeley met O. A. and
told him he was short of cash and needed to buy

on credit to stock his store.

O. A. asked Mr. Neeley how he liked Chestochina and the store. When Mr. Neeley replied that he liked it fine, O. A. looked at him and asked Mr. Neeley if he would like to buy the store. Mr. Neeley said he was already buying it from Mr. Rowland, having paid him $1,500, which put him in cash short position.

Then O. A. made Mr. Neeley a proposition which he couldn't refuse. O. A. told him that Mr. Rowland was only leasing the store from O. A. and had no right to sell it but that he would sell it to the Neeleys on condition that the Neeleys buy all their supplies from him and that after three years pay him $1,500 and the property would be theirs.

Taken aback by the shock of Mr. Rowland's double dealing, but relieved at such a magnanimous offer, Mr. Neeley could only but agree to O. A.'s terms. And according to his son, Sy, that's what happened.

What a terrific story!

# SPOOKS NOOK

O. A. Nelson and my mother, Mary Steelman, opened up the old Commercial Hotel in the summer of 1948 and renamed the place, Spooks Nook. It had been ten years since the railroad had pulled out, the mine had closed, and since everyone persisted in calling Chitina a ghost town O. A. figured he would make the place a real ghost town by painting large, white ghosts on the abandoned garages and barns and by renaming the old hotel.

The old place was in fairly good shape, considering that no one had used it for several years. O. A. re-did the plumbing and wiring so that the bathrooms and kitchen were operational and there were lights. He couldn't do anything about the settling. The hotel had been built on permafrost, and its main support beam held true down the middle, from front to rear, but the heat from the sun in the summer had melted the permafrost along the perimeter of the hotel causing it to settle into the ground. It hadn't settled evenly so O. A. did some shoring-up work where he could so the dining room, kitchen, the manager's apartment in the back, and the laundry room were pretty level, but the lobby gave cause for concern to even the most sober entrant.

The Commercial Hotel had been built in the early twenties and its 20 bedrooms had served part of the transient community well. It had been the smaller of two hotels in Chitina. The larger one, The Chitina Hotel, had burned down several years before. By opening Spooks Nook again, mother and O. A. intended to stand foursquare in the middle of the postwar Alaska summer tourist business. The few tourists came mainly from Anchorage.

The journey from Anchorage was a 256-mile

one-way drive on gravel roads. We rarely had to turn anyone away. Mom always seemed to make room at any time of the day or night. O. A. owned a couple of small houses a block away from the hotel where we could put extra people. Families would often rent those places for several days at a time.

I was Mother's only employee. I was her bullcook. My job was to split wood, clean bathrooms, mop floors, and change bed linens. I was quite busy on the weekends when most of the guests were there, as well as on Monday, when we did the heavy cleaning and the laundry. During the week I had a lot of time off, so I fishing for trout and grayling.

I particularly remember the three wood-burning stoves which I had to keep going. The main stove was a huge, old Lang kitchen range which cooked, baked, and fried everything served up family style in the 16-place dining room three times a day. We had two  sittings on the weekends. What a grand old device that kitchen stove was! Its surface had to be cured by rubbing it with a wool-wrapped salt block. And, believe it or not, the oven was perfectly true to its built-in thermometer. Its oven was as large as most modern home fireplaces.

The kitchen was the center of activity in the hotel and the gathering place for most of our visitors. The next, most vital, burner was a huge boiler stove in the laundry room in the back of the hotel. It was used to take care of the weekly accumulation of dirty linens. We fired  it up sporadically during the week for regular hot water but we stoked it early in the morning until late at night on Monday to do the laundry. The third stove was in the lobby and it was rarely used during the summer, but by late August and early September, before the hotel closed down for the winter, it was needed to cut down the nightly chill.

O. A. would haul in truckloads of cut wood
and dump them outside the back door of the hotel
near the kitchen for me to split.  I would split
at least a half a cord each day.  All Chitina
was heated by wood back then and
with winter temperatures at minus 50 or 60, it
was necessary to stockpile hundreds of cords of
wood in the fall.  The hotel cut into O. A.'s
wood supply considerably.

As a teenager, I became quite adept at
wood splitting.  I used a double-bitted axe and
once in a while used a maul and a splitting
wedge.  I only wish my golf stroke today was as
effective as my wood-splitting swing was then!

Folks who run hotels would probably all
agree that people are very different from each
other.  We would have been no exception to that
thinking.  Our little operation had some pretty
strange ducks staying with us during those two
seasons.  The strangest may have been an old
timer, a professional bullcook named Ben Pinks,
who showed up June 15, 1949, with the intention
of staying an entire month.  After about a week,
Mom couldn't wait for him to leave, but he
stayed the full time and made his mark by both
his presence and his stories.

Ben Pinks was a little fellow, about 65
years old, with gray hair wearing bent, dirty
glasses.  His face was kind of squinty.  And he
had an unusual deformity.  One of his legs was
severely bowed in a pronounced "C".  He told us
that when he came to Alaska on a sailing ship as
a young man, he fell and broke his leg during a
storm.  It healed and the bone knitted into its
"C"-shape due to the lousy job the crew did when
they set his leg.

He was a fixture in mining camps and road
maintenance camps throughout central Alaska as a
bullcook  We never figured out the reason he took
off a month in the middle of his normal work
period.  Mom didn't like him because he

holed up in his room, got real drunk, wet his
bed, and was loud and obnoxious as well.

But Ben Pinks renown had nothing to do
with his job or his drinking. Today's guardians
of Alaska would have put him in jail for life
because old Ben was a killer.

As he got drunker and drunker, he told us
over and over how he had killed more than 250
brown bears! He hated brown bears with a
viciousness which was hard to believe. Seems
that he and his partner were hiking along a
trail north of Fairbanks years before and a
brown bear had jumped his partner and killed him
on the spot. Ben never got over the loss of his
partner and whenever he got the chance he would
hunt down and kill as many bear that he could.
He would follow salmon streams up to where they
pooled and mow down any bear he found fishing in
these holes.

One day he came downstairs with a big,
double-barreled shotgun and told us the bear
story again and then, looking at me, said he
wanted to have a bang-up Fourth of July and
wanted me to be a part of it. He wanted me to
shoot his ten gauge shotgun the next day, which
was the 4th, so everyone could enjoy it. Well,
that seemed pretty exciting to me! I had never
seen a ten-gauge shotgun before and it looked
mammoth. I asked Mom if it would be all ight.
She told me to aim it out over the lake so I
wouldn't hit anybody.

On the morning of the 4th of July, Ben
Pinks handed me the shotgun and over 250 shells.
I can remember firing off the rounds two at a
time straight up into the air and the shot
pattern covering the entire lake. The recoil
padding was so good that there was only a
minimal kick when firing both barrels together.
Old Ben stayed up in the hotel and probably got
drunk because I didn't see him to give the
shotgun back until the following day.

I'm sure the noise bothered somebody. However,
I thought it was great!

The very first day that Spooks Nook was
opened in 1948, we handled a touring party from
Anchorage headed by Herb Hilscher. The group
had come in a large bus.

Mom brought in some help and we all worked
at this brand-new job, cooking, feeding,
cleaning and the like. The group left the next
day and stayed at Copper Center. This Hilscher-
led group worked on one of the military bases.
(Herb, a few years later gained quite a
reputation as a writer, historian, and
publicist). A couple of days after they left,
we got word that most of the group had fallen
ill from eating spoiled food. When it turned
out that salmonella was the culprit and that the
Copper Center Roadhouse had served it, we were
all vastly relieved. But, for a few days we
didn't know what was going to happen to us.
After that crisis, our business continued to do
well for the rest of the summer.

I don't know how he arranged it, but O. A.
got furniture for the rooms in the hotel from
the Kennecott Mine. Kennicott was 65 miles
away, across two rivers, and getting it from
there to Chitina had probably been done during
the winter before the ice went out. It would
have had to have been worked out with the
caretaker, Paul Wilhelm. There was no way that
the beds and chests would have been carried
across the Copper in the work box of the
elevated cable car. They were no doubt skidded
on the ice across the Kennicott River at
McCarthy, then towed down to Chitina on the old
railroad tracks by a speeder, and then hauled
across the ice at Chitina in a sledge pulled by
a Caterpillar tractor. Now that I think more
about it, O. A. got a pool table for his own
place from the Kennecott Mine at the same time.
I have a picture of him hoisting the pool table

upstairs through an outside window over the drug store.

Dinnertime at Spooks Nook was a kind of trap for our guests. Two things stand out, other than Mom cooking family style and the fact that there wasn't any menu, just good food.

O. A. had found a skull somewhere and had fastened it to a board with a magnet and a drycell battery so that when a circuit was completed in the kitchen the lower jaw clacked shut with a loud snap. He hung this trophy on the dining room wall behind the head of the table where he usually presided at mealtime. Sometime during dinner, he would give Mom the "high sign" and she would touch two wires together in the back stairs behind the dining room wall, and more than one tourist dropped his fork when he glanced up and saw Chief Joseph's skull talking. O. A. had given the relic the name of the famous plains Indian without any verification. O. A. would commandeer the head of the dinner table and then encourage any and all to participate in debating some topic of the day. Invariably, he would find out which stand a person favored on whatever subject it was, and then, perversely, he would argue the other side...and usually he would dominate and win the argument. It was all in good fun, of course. Dinner was an interesting time, and if there wasn't a crowd to prompt a second dinner setting, everyone tended to linger at the table to enjoy the camaraderie they found there.

All kinds of things happened in the hotel. Everything from epileptic seizures to people being total hogs at the table. One guest even fell down in one of the bedrooms and broke his arm. Another morning, two fellows sat down to eat breakfast and promptly divided a huge platter loaded with a dozen and a half scrambled eggs between them. They ate everything in sight and left without paying.

We figured out later that these were the same spoilers who practically fished out the second lake, leaving over a hundred grayling lying dead on its shore!

Opening the hotel was a great part of my growing up, because it took place during the last two summers before I graduated from high school. I got to spend a lot of quality time with my family and thus I met a wealth of interesting pioneers. After my folks left Chitina in early 1950 no one was left to run the hotel, so it closed for good. A few years later, it burned to the ground. If you go to Chitina some day, you might see where Spooks Nook was located by standing right in front of the old tin shop and looking south across the street toward the village. On a clear day, you will be able to see Spirit Mountain in the distance, but during 1948 and 1949 an old wreck of a building would have loomed large in front of you.

The hotel is gone but, in all likelihood, its ghosts are still in the adjoining neighborhood.

# CORDOVA GROUND SERVICE

This isn't meant to be a history of Cordova Air Service. Instead it will just mention highlights I remember about it during the late '40s. The little aviation company, owned and operated by Merle Smith, was truly a rag-tag outfit and merited the nickname, Cordova Ground Service, placed upon it by the trappers and prospectors who often saw the arrival of one of its planes several days after it was supposed to have picked them up to fly them elsewhere. These are just some of my memories of the airline from the time my dad started flying for "Smitty" until I left Cordova for college in 1950.

My stepfather, Hildreth "Pappy" Steelman, had flown in Alaska during World War II, and later he tried to make a success of his own flying service in Atlantic City, New Jersey. After that he flew for AAXICO, the American Air Export and Import Company, between San Juan, Puerto Rico, and New York City. Next he wrote to all the air operators in Alaska and "Smitty" offered him a job in Cordova. We arrived at the Mile 13 airport on a Pacific Northern Airlines DC-3 on July 11, 1947, and rode into town in a taxicab driven by "Pop" Helekel, who drove us up to the front door of the Cordova Air Service office on Main Street. Dad's job was to fly the beautiful, silver DC-3 which we had seen parked at Mile 13.

"Smitty" burst through the front doorway to shake Dad's hand, saying, "You must be Steelman. I just sold the three!"

Well, there we were. The only other multi-engined aircraft in Smitty's stable of old aircraft was a twin-engined Cessna which they never used. So, it was a completely different kind of plane with which Dad became

89

quickly acquainted. The next day he checked out in a float plane for the first time, and for the rest of the summer he flew around Prince William Sound from Valdez to Port Nellie Juan, and then down to Katalla and Yakataga.

In the meantime, Mom, my sister, Mary-Linda, and I got settled, First we rented the Red Cross cabin out on the Three Mile Bay Road from "Pop" Helekel for a month, and then we moved into town into a house on Ocean Dock Road, next door to Bill and Lois Zirglis. Lois was Bob Cunningham's sister and Bob and Helen owned and operated Cordova Drug on Main Street. While Dad was becoming acclimated to small-plane maritime work, I was making friends and Mom, along with Mary-Linda, was making a comfortable home for us.

But, in September, "Smitty" decided to send the folks to Chitina so Dad could operate the business there and keep up the mail runs in the Wrangell Mountains area. Uprooted again! The folks boarded me across the street with the Don Stettlers and they moved to Chitina. I would visit them during every available school vacation and then would spend the next two summers working for Mom in an old hotel she and O. A. Nelson re-opened.

Cordova Air Service! In 1947, "Smitty" only had two identical airplanes. They were two gull-winged Stinsons and they were the backbone of his operation. He also had a Stinson L-5, an old Stinson SM8A, a Norduyn Norseman, a staggered-wing Beechcraft, and a Taylorcraft, as well as the aforementioned twin Cessna. For those who recognize the concept of economics via standardization, such a mess would have skewered any aspirations for success.

Every one of the planes was convertible from wheels to floats except the Cessna and the Beech. "Smitty's" hangar was on the west shore of Lake Eyak at the city airport and that fresh-water lake held its ice well into spring, so when it came time to put some planes on floats, they would skid down the ramp from the hangar on-to the ice-covered lake on floats and then take off, landing at the city dock a half mile away in salt water. The reverse was done when the float planes needed extraordinary maintenance. Landing a float plane on the frozen lake took a lot more skill and care than taking off from the lake. Floats then and now are prohibitively expensive and a hard landing could easily have ruptured a weld and caused a leak.

None of the planes were instrumented for I.F.R. (instrument flight rules) flying and since the usual weather along the coast was overcast with mist, light rain, snow in the winter, and winds most of the time, flying V.F.R. (visual flight rules) required a lot of low-level trips and a strong knowledge of the varied terrain in order to complete the assortment of flights.

"Smitty" didn't get paid for incomplete flights. For example, during the heart of the winter of 1948-1949, my dad tried day after day to get a flight going from Chitina to McCarthy with mail and supplies. The temperature 131 miles away in Cordova was a balmy 42 degrees above zero while it was 50 below in Chitina! Regardless, "Smitty" was on the radio every day asking "Pappy" why he hadn't completed the flight.

The first day of that fateful week, Dad firepotted the old Dodge panel truck, got it started, loaded it, drove to One Mile Lake, firepotted the gull-winged Stinson, loaded the plane, and then he couldn't get it started. Because of the minimum amount of daylight and the extreme cold, he only had one chance to get this whole procedure to work. So, as soon as he couldn't get the plane started, he had to quickly reverse the process, drain the oil from the plane, unload it, reload the truck which he had kept going while seeing if the plane would start, and then take everything back to the Chitina Cash Store, unload it, and then go home.

The second day, Tuesday, the Dodge truck wouldn't start. The temperature never got any warmer than 50 below that entire week. And, it actually went to 60 below a couple of times.

The third day, Wednesday, was a repeat of Monday's efforts.

The fourth day, Thursday, was another Tuesday.

Finally, on Friday, Dad got it all working, and, after turning off the truck, he climbed back in the plane, taxied all the way to the north end of the lake, and started his take-off. He got airborne all right, but because the air was so cold and dense, he was unable to get the plane any higher than ten feet. Beyond the end of the lake, towards town, the ground drops off, so he knew he would be able to gain the altitude he needed at that point because the canyon opened up and he would be able to increase his airspeed. But just before he got to that point, about a hundred feet after leaving the end of the lake, the skis started clipping the sparse brush between the lake and the dropoff.

Unfortunately the brush was enough to pull the plane down, and it settled into the snow and bushes with a crash. Dad wasn't injured, but the plane had suffered enough damage to its skis, struts, undercarriage, and wings so that it wasn't flyable. Dad was really frustrated. To think! After all that work, he ended up with the only airplane crash he ever had in his life!

That was the last winter Dad flew for "Smitty". The airline's cash receipts were pretty slim those next few months before Dad finally went to Anchorage and caught on with

Bob Reeves and started flying multi-engines
again on the chain. "Smitty" didn't have any
money to pay Dad his salary, but had made
arrangements for the folks to continue charging
food and supplies at The Chitina Cash Store and
living rent free in the old Shepherd house. It
took a year and a half, until the summer of
1950, before "Smitty" and his maintenance crew
got the gull-wing flying again. They had to
truck it to Valdez and then take it to Cordova
on a power scow before they could even start to
repair it.

With today's more powerful equipment and
improved radio communications, it seems strange
to reflect on the lack of capability in the
small-plane flying services of fifty years ago.
The weather is the same, the temperatures just
as cold, and the pilots and mechanics just as
dedicated. The big difference lies in the
equipment. But C. A. S. flew to some fantastic
places regularly and those pilots doing it
shrugged off their accomplishments as a matter
of course. Take Chisana, for example. (That's
pronounced Shoo sha na.) The place is located
beyond Skolai and White Passes in the heart of
the Wrangell Mountains and was the site of a
gold rush in the 1920's. Its airstrip was at a
high elevation. Landing was into a mountain
going uphill, and taking off was away from the
mountain, downhill. It was critical flying.
Most of the strips, gravel bars, and other
unimproved patches they used were not much
better.

Dad landed the L-5 Stinson short at the
McCarthy field one winter day, and the brush at
the end of the runway cut open the fabric
underbody of the fuselage and snow jammed inside
the cone of the fuselage and tail
assembly so badly that he couldn't take off. It
took him more than four hours to chip away
the ice and frozen snow and patch the hole in

93

the fabric so he could fly back to Chitina. It
was below zero then, so I'm not sure how he
patched the fabric. There was no duct tape back
then. It's a wonder anyone was able to repair
anything without the duct tape we have today.

Flying was an all-consuming love of Dad,
and it was probably the same with the rest of
the crew who flew for "Smitty", as well as with
"Smitty" himself. The men would do anything to
keep the air service going. They'd fly
anywhere and haul anything. "Smitty" had a
government contract with the Alaska Road
Commission to resupply its small operation up
the Chitina River valley at May Creek. They
were doing road and airport maintenance in that
area with a D-8 Cat and a dump truck. So, to
support this, the Norseman was moved up from
Cordova to haul drums of gasoline. Dad had me
help him load those large drums into that old
workhorse. We could load five drums of fuel in
its cabin. These were standard 55-gallon
drums. At six pounds a gallon, plus the weight
of the metal drum, it meant hauling a dead
weight of nearly a ton. The old plane didn't
jump off the runway with such a load. In fact
it rose very slowly into the air. But, each
summer, at least 50 drums of gas was flown up to
May Creek that way.

I'm sure the C. A. A., now renamed the
F. A. A., turned a blind eye many times toward
"Smitty's" Cordova Air Service. Alaska was
still a territory then and there weren't many
air operators competing for the precious little
business there was, so the small crew of C. A.
A. inspectors were centered in Anchorage and
Fairbanks. Engines were overhauled and aircraft were inspected by company A & E's who
signed off the maintenance.

When required, the planes were ferried to
Anchorage for major work by Reeve Airmotive.
The system seemed to work well, but I remember

94

one exception.  They had just got the old
Stinson SM8A back from Reeve and on its very
first flight the engine stopped cold.  Larry "the
General" Barr had to land it on the delta sands
next to the Eyak River, not six miles away from
its takeoff at the city airport.  Quicksand
still has the plane.  No one was ever able to
retrieve it, and the plane sunk completely into
the sand in less than three days.  Reeve never
gave "Smitty" a rebate for its work either!

Christmas of 1949, Dad had a flight on
Christmas Eve to Tebay Lake to leave supplies
for a trapper.  Close to the shortest day of the
year, there was minimum daylight.  It was a
relatively short hop across the Copper River and
into the Hanagita Range.  But daylight
disappeared and Dad still hadn't returned.  We
were really worried.  There was no ground-to-air
radio set up, so we were in the dark about where
Dad was.  Finally, at least three hours after he
should have returned, he flew over the town and
we raced out to the lake to pick him up.

He almost didn't make it back!  When he
had flown to Tebay Lake, there was no sign of
the trapper, so Dad landed on the lake and
carried all of the supplies up to the cabin by
himself.  The snow was pretty deep and, by the
time he got back to the plane, the temperature
had risen and the plane had mushed down in the
snow.  Dad got out the  snowshoes and tramped
out a runway in the soft snow so he could take
off.  He was flying the Stinson L-5 on skis.  He
got back in the plane and roared down the
tramped-out track.  But he hadn't made the
runway long enough and ran out of space without
getting airborne.  So he got out again and
tramped a much longer strip.  He couldn't turn
the plane around to use the strip he had
already made because of the weight of the plane
and the drag of the skis, so it meant that he
had to tramp out another complete strip.  He

tried to take off again, only to end up the
same way as the first time.  Just not enough
packed snow!

By then, it had become darker and he was
getting tired, but he knew that he had to get
out of there because the temperature would only
get colder as it got later, and if he didn't fly
soon he would end up stuck, frozen in the snow.
So, he tramped out another strip and got all set
again to take off, for the third time.  But the
temperature had indeed fallen while he was
making the third runway and the skis of the L-5
had frozen to the snow!  Dad's only hope then
was to open the throttle full, get out of the
plane, go back to the tail, and shove it up and
down to make the skis  crack loose from the
frozen snow.

He did it and this time his plan worked!

All of a sudden, the plane lurched
forward.  Dad barely leapt on the skis, and
somehow clambered into the cockpit and took off.
If he hadn't managed to fly on that third
attempt, Dad would have spent Christmas at Tebay
Lake.  Due to the weather and temperature
changes, we figured that he might even have been
there for at least another week before anybody
could have flown him out.  It might have been
much longer!

Characters abounded back then.  Both the
people living in Chitina seemed larger than life
as well as the passengers and folks living in
those remote areas.  There was a couple living
in McCarthy named Blanch Smith and Ernie
Gherkin.  Ernie had saved Blanch's life in the
McCarthy fire.  In 1949 she was in her 70's.
Ernie was not much younger.  For those of you
with long memories, Ernie Gherkin was the
spittin' image of the cartoon character in the
Dick Tracy comic strip known as B. O. Plenty.
Blanch took a special liking to my Dad and, when
she knew he was flying to McCarthy,

nothing would do but he had to take time to stop down at their place for some apple pie. Dad loved pie for breakfast and would have eaten it every morning, so I don't believe he ever passed up the "best pie in the Chitina River Valley".

Blanch Smith jokingly called herself "the first white woman in Dawson". She had been a "sporting lady" during the gold rush and she had been the first, non-native woman to live there. She was gorgeous and she was of African descent.

The famous Alaskan painter, Fred Machetanz, produced a work called "Eighty Seasons" which is a face of an old sourdough ringed with a great beard and bushy hair. Dad actually flew the model for this painting around. He was just as Mr. Machetanz had captured him on canvas. His name was George Schmock, and Dad not only flew Mr. Schmock but all of his dogs too. One time, there were 13 dogs and puppies to take somewhere, and there just wasn't enough room for all of them, or maybe they made a deal. Anyway, Dad became the owner of a fledgling sled dog named Nig. The folks gave Nig to George Nagengast when they left Chitina. However, earlier we kept the dog in the back yard. Then we shot and froze rabbits and dried a lot of salmon to feed him. Dad decided to make a sled so Nig could be his one-dog team. That enterprise led to a disaster!

Dad had almost finished the sled. He was smoothing the runners with a drawknife which is operated by pulling it towards ones body. A drawknife is a two-handled knife with a broad, sharp blade. There was a knot on the runner and when Dad braced the end of the runner with his knee...you guessed it...the knife cut through the knot, kept on coming, and sliced through his stretched knee, easily going through his work pants and long johns. The

knee popped open across its front where the
kneecap protrudes. Mom quickly taped it up and,
since Dad was hobbled and needed to be off his
feet for awhile, went down to the drugstore and
radioed Cordova that he'd had an accident and
would be out of action for a few days.    While
she was away, Dad hopped over to the cupboard in
the kitchen and pulled a bottle of whiskey from
the top shelf in the kitchen cabinet and poured
himself a stiff drink. I watched him do it.
And, no sooner had he drank the whiskey, he went
into shock! He was out of action for much
longer than a few days. I think that drink kept
Dad off his feet for over a week. What lesson
did Dad learn? He learned not to drink after
being injured. Coming inside from 40 below zero
to 70 above, getting cut, and then drinking,
meant that too many things had happened at once.
His body hadn't stood a chance to adjust to
those stresses.

        "Smitty" operated Cordova Air Service for
a long time after my Dad left his employment.
Both became much friendlier after Dad went to
work for somebody else.  "Smitty" was an out-
rageous character in his own right.  The air
service almost folded in the late spring of
1950.  Dad was flying for Reeve Aleutian Airways
by then, I was in school in Cordova, and Mom and
Mary-Linda were still in Chitina.  I kept in
touch with Mom through C. A. S. at its office on
Main Street, Cordova.  I knew times were tough
for "Smitty" because during one two-week period
almost everyone of his planes had an accident!
The Beechcraft ran
into some pilings in the Valdez small-boat
harbor.  The Stinson SM8A crash-landed in the
Eyak River flats and sank in the sand.  The
other planes either collided with one another or
had serious, expensive mishaps.  Things were a
mess!

        One day, coincidentally, I was in the air

98

service office when "Smitty" opened a letter from the U. S. Post Office. It was an official letter giving Cordova Air Service contracts to fly the mail from Cordova to Katalla and Yagataga. These two routes had been flown by "Smitty" without pay for over two years. And, also in the envelope, was a government check for back mail pay in the amount of $15,000.00!

Smitty never looked back after that. Cordova Air Service went on to become Cordova Airlines, flying Convairs along the Alaskan gulf coast, and eventually merging with Alaska Coastal-Ellis Airlines and Alaska Airlines. Alaska bought out the two smaller carriers and captured the entire coastal market from Anchorage to Ketchikan, absorbing several experienced airline managers in the process. These men, Shell Simmons, Ben Beneke, and Bob Ellis, helped vitalize Alaska Airlines to its present prominence in the western United States.

Fifteen Thousand Dollars in 1950 was a small fortune! Dad only made $500 a month when he flew for "Smitty". To put that amount into perspective today, $15,000 would now be worth close to $150,000!

One last thing. In those days Merle Smith was usually called "Smitty". Some of the oldtimers called him "Smithy". However, he didn't become the legendary "Mudhole Smith" until much later. But "Smitty" and his Cordova Air Service were both regarded with great affection by all who knew of them.

# VISITORS

After leaving New Jersey, we only had relatives visit us once. My grandmother and step-grandfather drove up from Montara, California, during the summer of 1949. Alice Osman, a family friend, came to Chitina from Atlantic City at the same time. Dad was able to come back from flying for Reeve, and he and Mom enjoyed their visit immensely, as did I.

I had lived with my grandparents from kindergarten until the start of the fourth grade in Ocean City and Somers Point, New Jersey, until shortly after my grandfather died. My grandmother, Linda Bowen, who was my mother's mother, married Mr. Paul Schiable. She and Paul had been engaged to marry in 1902, but her father forbade her to go west to California and marry Paul because her dad believed she would be going to a violent land. The 1902 earthquake proved his assertion to be correct.

Thus she married Laurence Bowen, raised a family, became a grandmother several times, was widowed, and then married her girlhood sweet-heart. Paul had been married twice, widowed once and divorced once. He traveled back to New Jersey often and always stopped by my grandmother to visit. I was told that my granddad told Linda that if he should leave this earth before her, she should to marry Paul, because he was a good man. After grand-pa's death, Paul and my grandmother renewed their romance and enjoyed over twenty years together.

They drove a Fraser to Chitina and back. Gravel roads made for hard driving and they stayed for almost a month. Paul broke out the horseshoes and challenged anyone who might want to play a game. Grandmom helped Mom in the kitchen but mostly they all just visited, traveled around, flew here and there, saw the country, and delighted one another by just being together for awhile.

It seemed vitally important to me to see Grandmother again because she had been my surrogate mom when I lived with her in Somers Point. Mom kept an apartment in Atlantic City in the same place where Alice Osman lived and came back to Somers Point two or three times a month. She was working at Soloff's restaurant. It was while she was there that she met my future stepfather, Hildreth Steelman.

Grandmom was an old-fashioned cook. She could cook anything. Had recipes, of course, but they often proved not to be exact. One of my favorites was her lemon meringue pie. I often asked my mom to bake one. Her pie production was pretty good but somehow it never tasted as good as Grandmom's. Finally, she wrote to Grandmom and asked her for a recipe for the pie. After getting it, she baked a pie for me. It was markedly better but it still wasn't the same. So, when Grandmom came to visit, Mom and I both asked her to make a lemon meringue pie. Mom dangled the recipe in front of her and then watched.

Grandmom never looked at the recipe. She just started putting ingredients together. Instead of two eggs she used four. Instead of a cup and a half of sugar, two and a half cups. And, so on!

The pie was perfect!

By this time, Paul was 71 and Grandmom was 63. They visited me once while I was a sophomore in college at Oregon State in Corvallis. That was the last time I saw them.

O. A. Nelson had been married, but his wife couldn't tolerate living in Chitina. She moved away, taking their two adopted children. However, she left their natural son, Adrian, with his father. Adrian was a brilliant young man who graduated from Thomas Edison's school in New Jersey. When Adrian returned to Chitina he and O. A. built a direct current power plant on the bank of the Copper River.

Unfortunately, Adrian contracted Bright's Disease and died at the age of 27. We never met him as he died earlier in the year my folks moved to Chitina, in 1947.

The next summer, Ora, one of O. A.'s adopted daughters came to visit O. A. She brought a friend named Judy Schloss with her from back East. Having Ora visit was good for O. A. and he spent many hours showing the girls the country. They flew and drove everywhere they could for about a month. One day we all went swimming in One Mile Lake. That was the only time I ever went swimming in Chitina.

Alice Osman had been a long-time friend of my stepfather's sister, Betty Force. Alice had been faithfuly squired by Aunt Betty's star boarder, Owen Leher, for many years. She was a schoolteacher. Coming all the way from the east coast and California was a mammoth trip to undertake.

Visits from relatives and friends were at a premium. There were but few of them and they were well remembered.

# DISASTERS

Alaska is no stranger to companies going out of business or to economies being shattered by strife, politics, or economic downturns. In the short ten years after the Kennecott Copper Mine and its attendant, Copper River and Northwestern Railway, went out of business the country reclaimed much of the serenity and natural way which had been there before 1900, when only a few Indians lived in this vast area. The few, remaining white people who still lived in Chitina and McCarthy continued to talk about the mine and the railroad. But, by the time we came on the scene, the survivors had seemingly long since gotten over any despair or recriminations and were engrossed in just being a part of the remote lifestyle. It was a way of living vastly scaled down from the hustling 1930's and was mostly just fine for the people still living there.

Today, our state faces a besieged bottom fishery in the Aleutians, another damaged salmon run in Bristol Bay, an extinct logging economy in southeast with both pulp mills being closed, as well as the never-ending ups and downs of the oil business. We have seen gold strikes come and go, a war economy grip the territory twice, a tremendous flood in central Alaska, as well as the greatest earthquake in modern times. And there continues to be the exhausting battle between ultra liberals and arch conservatives throughout the country. Both use Alaska as a political football in the game of national politics.

And, don't forget the Exxon Valdez calamity, which has set the tone for any ocean oil spill anywhere in the world!

No, we're no strangers to "boom and bust". The closures of the Kennecott Mine and its railroad turned Cordova from the richest per capita town or city in the world to a humble fishing village.

Only 131 miles away from Cordova lies little Chitina, which had served for a time as the starting point for shipping supplies into the interior of Alaska. This business stopped when the federal government built its own railroad from Seward to Fairbanks in 1916. I doubt that the government even considered the negative impact on the existing supply business it ruined before building the Alaska Railroad. Later on, in 1938, after a combination of rising costs of operation and a severe labor dispute, the owners decided to shut down the richest copper mine in the world. Kennecott was a high-grade copper mine with ore of more than 60% copper.

If you think that a thousand pulp mill employees out of a population of 15,000 losing their jobs in Ketchikan was a tragedy, imagine what a work force of 1,000 out of a population of 2,000 meant to the combined towns of Cordova, Chitina, McCarthy and Kennicott! It brought a wipeout!

So, you can see it is distinctly possible to use the word "disaster" as a synonym for the word "history" in dealing with Alaska. This would definitely be true for Chitina, Alaska, as well.

# THE LAST CHRISTMAS TRIP

Between November of 1947 and January of 1950, I flew home to Chitina six times for holidays and summer vacations.  The Christmas trip of 1949 was the most harrowing.

A broad, low-pressure system lay across Prince William Sound for the better part of three weeks and dumped an unusual amount of snow everywhere, keeping air traffic to a minimum. During one three-day period it snowed 12 feet in Valdez.  The snow level rose higher than the eaves of the houses!

I was the perennial "stand-by" passenger. "non-rev" in airline terminology.  The plan was always for me to ride on a business flight when traveling between Cordova and Chitina.  The system generally worked well except for this one time.

After a couple of days delay for mechanical reasons, or because there were other flights to fly which had greater priority, I was told someone would finally take me to Chitina via Valdez.  Starbuck was the pilot, and we were to fly in one of the gull-winged Stinsons.  We took off from the Lake Eyak City Airport, got halfway to Valdez, and then had to return because of a magneto problem.  We com-pleted the flight and landed in Valdez even though its airport had just received a half a foot of snow. The sun was shining and the flying weather was promising.  We dropped off the mail and cargo and quickly took off again, flying over Thompson Pass and following the Richardson Highway into the interior.  The good weather continued, but Starbuck decided that there was no way he was going to be able to fly all the way down to Chitina.  So, instead of turning south and following the Edgerton Cutoff down the Copper River from the Richardson, we

turned left which was north, and flew toward the
Gulkana Airport.  Starbuck radioed ahead, got
clearance to land at Gulkana, asked the
C. A. A. controller if anyone was driving down
to Copper Center, or better yet, Chitina.

Remembering back, there just wasn't any
other reason to take me up to that area except
that I had to get home for Christmas.  Measuring the trip on paper, Starbuck flew one half of
a round trip between Cordova and Valdez, about
60 miles, and then a full round trip from
Cordova to Gulkana via Valdez, another 370
miles.  He had to have flown 430 miles that day
to honor the company's promise to get me home in
time for Christmas!

But, I still wasn't home.  In fact, I was
55 miles from home.  It was two o'clock in the
afternoon, nearly dark, and I had no planned way
to get to Chitina.

Fortunately, the C. A. A. controller had
found someone who was driving down to Copper
Center and soon after Starbuck flew away I was
headed to Copper Center with a nice man in a
warm pickup truck.  The temperature was around
35 below.  That's why being warm was important.

We got to Copper Center and went into the
Copper Center Roadhouse. My driver started
asking everyone to learn if anyone was driving
to Chitina.  Well, we finally heard that there
were a couple of men who were down the street,
in a little bar, and they might be going.  The
gentleman went into the bar and found the two
men and, again fortune smiled on me.  We
arranged for me to ride with them when they
left.

About a half hour later the three of us
piled into an old, black sedan and drove south.
By this time, it was pitch black and the temperature had fallen to about 45 below.  I sat
alone in the back seat, shivering in spite of
being all wrapped up with the heavy clothes I

had been wearing all day and pulled an old blanket around me which I had found on the floor. It seemed like that 40-mile trip lasted forever.

My two benefactors were having a great time. They'd had a few drinks and for one of them it was also a homecoming. He had just been discharged from the army. The driver was Patty King and the ex-soldier was Johnny Billum. Winter drive, frigid temperatures, a narrow winding road, and my companions having had a few drinks really scared me. I was just 17. When we finally got to Chitina and the fellows took me to our house, I was the happiest and most relieved kid in the world!

We had started out around eight o'clock that morning in Cordova and it was close to ten that night when my long journey ended. Everyone I came into contact with that day helped me. Nobody wanted anything in return. Maybe it was just the Christmas spirit, but back then it seemed that everyone cared and helped out more than they do today.

"Spooks Nook" Hotel Opened in 1948

Lobby, Dining Room in rear at left

Chitina, circa 1943, Spirit Mt. in distance

Lifeline of the Wrangell Mts., 12/23/48

Otto A. Nelson, Hildreth "Pappy" Steelman and Sister Mary-Linda Steelman

Macabre Greeting to Tourists

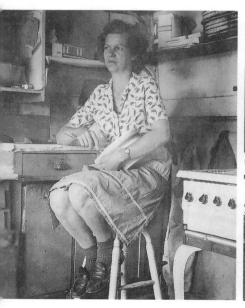

Mary Steelman

Abandoned Tin Shop

Gull-winged Stinson
and Jack Richards

Stinson SM8A and
Herb Haley

Pappy Steelman and
Bill Berry

Norduyn Norseman

Tram Across the Copper River

Converted Model T Speeder
and Paul Wilhelm

Tram Station and Stairs

Mom and Mary-Linda

O. A. Nelson and Pool Table

Dipnetting Salmon at the Point
Summer, 1949

Copper River Fishwheel

# THE LYON'S DEN

The finest log home for hundreds of miles around had been built by O. A. Nelson's sister and brother-in-law, Mabel and Jim Lyon. The house was located two blocks uphill from the drug store and enjoyed a commanding view of the town. I don't remember the type of logs with which the place had been built but, in looking back, they must have been imported because they were quite a lot bigger than any of the trees in the hills around Chitina. The building was a fully modernized house with indoor plumbing and a wood furnace in the basement, a large main floor with a full living room across the front of the house, a kitchen, a bath and a main bedroom downstairs. Upstairs was another large bedroom and a bull pen for visitors, bachelors and other passers-through. It had beautiful hardwood floors, which gave the home a finished look.

There was a huge, rock fireplace in the living room on an inside wall. The time my folks stayed there, they lighted the fireplace and, much to their dismay, discovered that fireplaces, in 40 below weather, sucked all the heat out of a house through the chimney. The problem compounded itself because they found out that should they let the fire die away, the house got so cold it took most of a full day to get it tolerably heated again. Once the logs in the fireplace began to burn, the only way to vent the smoke was up the chimney whose draft, even at a nearly closed setting, still pulled most of the heat in the house through the firebox and chimney.

And, even though the house was well built with marvelously crafted and fitted logs, every little hole or crack was an opening for a long finger of ice to form from the below zero air

outside.  This showplace was built on bedrock
and it is still there, although the weeds and
scrub brush have started to envelop it.  It's
actually hard to find now!

As with everything else in the townsite of
Chitina, the Lyon's Den was owned by O. A..  He
included it in his domestic hot water system
which was located in the basement of the drug
store.  Tap water was heated in a huge, wood-
fired boiler under the drug store and was piped
to four houses plus The Chitina Cash Store and,
in the summer, the old hotel.  Considering that
Chitina was a remote village and those were the
late forties, having this convenience in the
dead of a 40 to 60 below winter was pretty
special!  That same group of places also had
electric power from the direct current power
plant down at the river.

I only stayed in the Lyon's Den for one
holiday.  The temperatures were in the sub 60's
and as frigid and uncomfortable as it was, the
aura of that place was so pleasant and warm that
just thinking about it now, years later, makes
me grateful that I was able to stay in it even
for a short while.

Elsewhere, in writing about Chase, the
manager of the Chitina Cash Store, I recall that
Mabel Lyon returned to Chitina, her husband Jim
having died, and that she and Chase married and
moved away.  So O. A. ended up with no Chase in
The Cash Store as well as no Lyon in the Lyon's
Den.

## IDOLS ARE HUMAN

Toward the end of my second summer in Chitina, when the days were getting noticeably darker, and school wasn't that far away, several of us were gathered at The Cash Store one night when an unpleasant episode occurred. Chase was there with O. A. and Jack Richards, another person and me. All of a sudden three native ladies came in, and after a very short time, began to rank on O. A., talking pretty gross, mainly about him, but about others too, saying that the men wanted to screw them and that they had done so in the past. The "f" word was used a lot. The ladies got pretty mean and loud. It was obvious they were drunk and also pretty obvious they didn't much care for O. A.

Well, to me, O. A. was pretty special. Everything in the town was his. He was the main influence there. It was his store, he had been the deputy commissioner, and he was still the postmaster. All of a sudden, O. A. hauled off and drove his fist into the stomach of the loudest and most obnoxious of the three, doubling her up so much that she fell to the floor. I was dumbfounded! I just couldn't believe what I had seen. In the first place, I had never seen anyone hit a woman before in my life. In the second place, I didn't know what to do, so I didn't do or say anything.

The ladies left right away and the older men went about their business. Soon after I left and went home. It has been 49 years since then, and I am still shocked by what happened. No explanation or apology was ever tendered. In my opinion, what O. A. did was neither humane or necessary. My later experiences cause me to think that O. A. was either embarrassed, annoyed, or infuriated. Possibly, all three of these emotions.

That he might have had carnal knowledge with the lady was possible. Lust will out, they say. But I cannot remember ever seeing anything more brutal in my life than O. A. hitting that woman in the stomach. It is still hard to swallow the bitter pill which fell from the fist of my fallen idol that night.

I never told my folks what I had seen, and this is the first I've have related the story. So, this unexpected brutality is a picture of the cruel side of someone I idolized and respected immensely and told you about in a short biography, earlier in this journal.

# FIRST CHRISTMAS -1947

The wood stove in the little trackwalker's shack was cherry-red from its fire and
even though I was hovering over it, I was colder
than I had ever been in my life.  It was 50
below zero, we had just landed at One Mile Lake
near Chitina after flying up the Copper River
from Cordova, and I had come home for Christmas
from high school.  Less than a month earlier, I
had been in Chitina for Thanksgiving Vacation,
but that had been during a Chinook, and the
temperature difference between the two dates was
eighty degrees!  The light warmth of the old
plane translated to a frigidity in that little
shack which chills me to the bone even now when
I remember it.

I could have been wearing the downiest of
down coats and the toastiest of arctic mukluks,
and my mind would not have let me be warm!
There was no sun.  It was white and gray and
black outside.  The shortest day of the year was
the very next day, and we had been in the air
under a gray, forbidding canopy of clouds
overlaying the entire flight from Cordova.  It
was already getting dark as we unloaded the
plane.  Dad shooed me inside the shack to get
warm because he obviously recognized that I was
absolutely freezing.

When you are not prepared for that kind of
cold, dry as it might be, nothing, no nothing,
can warm you up!

Fortunately, we piled into the old Dodge
panel truck shortly afterward and went home.
Mom and Mary-Linda were there.  The house was
nice and warm and Mom made me some hot chocolate
and sat me near the woodstove so I could get
warm.  Before I went outside again, we changed a
lot of the clothes I wore, the footwear
especially, so I might regain my

minor place in the human race, instead of posing as an iceberg.

Christmas was great! We had a tree and stockings. My little sister got two baby kittens and I remember giving my folks a cigarette ashtray stand which I had made in manual training. It was painted to look like a toy soldier. Several oldtimers joined us for Christmas dinner, and we all visited around town with the few folks still living there.

I stayed in Chitina until after New Year's day and then flew back to Cordova where I was boarding with Don and Dorothy Stettler, their three kids, and a dog on Ocean Dock Road. When we left Chitina, it had warmed all the way up to 45 below but it was 75 degrees warmer in Cordova! It felt like a heat wave. Even though it had been wonderful to go to Chitina and visit my family, I was really glad to get out of that freezer and get warm again!

# THE ROAD OUT

Chitina is exactly 131 miles from Cordova by the old railroad and 131 miles from Valdez by the Richardson Highway and the Edgerton Cutoff. We mentioned before that the bulk of the inventory for The Chitina Cash Store was shipped to Chitina from Valdez, but we hadn't mentioned the other lifeline we enjoyed back then. It stretched from Anchorage to Chitina. Cliff Steadman operated a one-truck business called Interior Freight and drove from Anchorage and his home in Mountain View to Chitina and back every week. His brother-in-law, Bill Curran, drove a limo over in the summer and off and on during the winter, depending on how much people traffic he had.

At that time, there were several roadhouses still open along the Glenn and Richardson Highways. Only a few of them operate today. They were spaced along the road by the approximate distance it took for a team of horses and a wagon to travel in one day. With the advent of the motorcar, the roadhouses fell by the wayside. The expansion and improvement of those two highways, plus the addition of the Tok Cutoff, were more than enough reason for the Alaska Road Commission to relocate from Chitina to Glennallen.

During my first summer as a bullcook, I got to take two trips away from Chitina. One was to an Air Scout Encampment at Fort Richardson, after which I had to stay almost an extra week with the Steadmans in Mountain View because I missed the limo. The other was a trip all the way to Edmonton with Fred Coleclough. Fred was a retired tinsmith from Valdez. He was a widower and had been married to one of O. A. Nelson's sisters. He was taking his brother, George, to the train in

Edmonton on his way home to Toronto. Mom let me go with them and we had a great trip.

Highlights for me were swimming at the hot springs at Mile 497 near the Upper Liard River Bridge and seeing Edmonton again. We had lived there three years earlier during the last year of World War II, when my dad was flying in the Air Transport Command. The entire trip to Edmonton was on gravel roads. The folks in the Road Commission firmly maintained that gravel roads were better in Alaska than paved roads because of our freezing conditions, and that they could repair a pot boil or a permafrost collapse a lot easier with gravel roads. They said that paved roads would just buckle and be too expensive to build and keep repaired.

Take a look at the condition of the paved highway system in interior Alaska today and tell me that they weren't correct. Cost to build? High. Cost to re-build? High. Cost to repair? High. I venture that the overall cost of our road system, converting it to pavement, rebuilding them over and over, as well as the cost of repairs, has far exceeded the cost levels of a gravel highway system. But, we used 90% federal highway money, so who cares besides me?

We made the trip to and from Edmonton in a 1947 Dodge Hydramatic four-door sedan. It was a brand-new car and the trip was completed without any breakdown or real problems until we got almost home. We saw brown bear, moose, caribou, and all kinds of smaller game and birds, had a taste of traveling through a widely-spread forest fire in British Columbia, and stayed in a variety of camps and motels along the way.

Copper Center is only about 45 miles from Chitina and, when we finally got there on our way back, we stopped and Fred decided to have a drink at a little bar. After Fred had a few drinks, we got underway again.

We were about ten miles from Chitina when
the right front wheel of the Dodge caught a soft
shoulder and we ended up in the ditch.  Perhaps
Fred hadn't needed a drink after all.   We went
back to the car the next day and O. A. helped
Fred pull the Dodge out of the ditch.   There was
enough room in O. A.'s truck but we luckily were
picked up by Joe Goodlataw and rode into town in
the back of his pickup truck, a better choice.

I had forgotten all about Joe Goodlataw
until his obituary was published in 1997 in the
Anchorage Daily News.  We had called him Chief
and knew him as a well-liked person who always
smiled and was known as a hard worker.  The
obituary said that he had been born in the
abandoned village of Taral which lay across the
Copper River from Chitina on the east bank about
ten miles south.  Chief Goodlataw died when  he
was  96 and was survived by three daughters,
three sons, 31 grandchildren, 62 great-
grandchildren,  and five great-great-
grandchildren.  He had been predeceased by his
two wives and eight of his children.

Joe  had  worked  for  the Alaska Road
Commission from 1920 to 1953, ten hours a day
for as little as 32 cents an hour.  One of his
other jobs included transporting people from
Chitina to Valdez and then to Fairbanks in a
Model T Ford.  When  the  car broke down, he
often had to walk long distances.  However his
treks from Gulkana to Chitina, some eighty miles
were of no concern to him.

A few years later, during my first year in
college, his daughter, Mae, made a point of
stopping to talk with me after our basketball
game against the Sitka ANB at Mt. Edgecumbe.
She was attending the B. I. A. boarding school
there.  I saw Mae again in Palmer years later,
but I never saw Joe Goodlataw after the time he
helped us after the accident.

I drove back to Chitina several times

over the following years. But the most memorable time was when I went there after finishing up a construction job one summer. I hitch-hiked over from Palmer to see O. A. Nelson. Three separate times I got rides just in time to avoid serious confrontations with large, wild animals: a bull moose, a buffalo cow and calf, and a brown bear, lying full length across the road at twilight time, stretched out like a poodle with the tips of his front and back claws touching the shoulders on both sides of the road.

Today, most of the people, going to Chitina or passing through it on their way to McCarthy, are tourists. The road has been improved. There are several long straight stretches on the Edgerton now instead of the never-ending winding road it used to be. For the most part, the drive is all right. The road has been spoiled, however along One Mile Lake. The road builders laid a straight stretch along the east side of the lake and it looks and feels like a scar against the former beauty it runs by. The old road wound along the west side and was more in keeping with the beauty of the lake.

Times change.

# AND, TODAY

The only bar burned to the ground a year ago because the firefighting equipment was frozen. The temperatures were under 50 below. Even the Kenny Lake firefighters from 30 miles away couldn't help. The valves on their equipment had frozen. The water source, a pond nearby, was too dry to be of any use.

People flock to Chitina in the summer to dip for salmon on a permit basis from the state.

The Indian village is almost non-existent.

The picturesque, winding, narrow road has been replaced with tangents up to 20 miles long, straight as dies, barren scars on the fragile landscape. A monster of a road smears the east side of One Mile Lake, and is now located on the other side of the lake from the original road.

Hyundai Corporation built a permanent bridge across the Copper River in the early 1970's, over 30 years after the railroad shut down. Fine silt drifts along the railings and the deck of the bridge like a light-brown snowfall.

Up river, above the bridge, one can count the remnants of more than ten abandoned fishwheels cluttering the eastern shoreline.

Up from the shore, extending eastward for a few miles, the native corporation has logged the virgin stands of spruce which had died from an infestation of spruce bark beetles.

Former Governor Walter Hickel attempted to build a Copper River Highway down the river towards the coast from Chitina. This effort was stopped by a host of organizations, including the native village corporation, and Ahtna, its parent native corporation, various environmental groups, as well as a strident public outcry. The governor was having the Department of Transportation bulldoze a pioneer road along the old railroad right-of-way without securing proper permiting or with little consideration for any of the archeological sites of the natives along the route.

The present population of Chitina seems to consist of a battery of escapists. People who wouldn't live anywhere else in the world. They are the same kind of folks who lived there 50 years ago when I was there!